The Slate Railways of Wales

Alun John Richards

ISBN: 0-86381-689-4

Cover design: Sian Parri

The publishers acknowledge that two of the inside illustrations are
courtesy Crown copyright, RCAHM Wales – Rokeby Collection:
Tal-y-llyn Railway, Abergynolwyn Station;
Welsh Highland Railway, Porthmadog New Station.

First published in 2001 by
Gwasg Carreg Gwalch, 12 Iard yr Orsaf, Llanrwst, Wales LL26 0EH
☎ 01492 642031   🖷 01492 641502
✆ books@carreg-gwalch.co.uk   Internet: www.carreg-gwalch.co.uk

Cover illustration:
Ffestiniog Railway locomotive Iarll Meirionnydd leaving
Blaenau Ffestiniog station. Photo author.

Back-cover illustrations:
Author at the Welsh Slate Museum riding the motorcycle adapted to run
on rails underground for the use of the manager of Oakeley quarry,
Blaenau Ffestiniog.

The Cob, Traeth Mawr, Porthmadog, 1810 H.W. Billington.
Courtesy National Library of Wales.
(View from Ynys Tywyn during construction.)

Dedicated to:
DAFYDD PRICE 1921-2000

Richard Pennant, the Right Honourable Baron Penrhyn of Penrhyn in the County Lough, is popularly reviled as a thief of land and the founder of a harsh and exploitive dynasty. However it is due to his enterprise, energy and foresight that on 25th June 1801, for the first time, slates were carried from a quarry to a seaport not in a cart, nor on the back of an animal or of a man, but on rails.

The Author

Alun John Richards has spent over thirty years studying the history, methods and transport of the Welsh slate industry. His work as an engineer brought him into contact with the active North Wales quarries, where he was responsible for several technical innovations.

He was for many years a Guest Tutor on the Slate Industry at the Snowdonia National Park Study Centre at Plas Tan-y-bwlch, and sometime lecturer at Coleg Harlech Summer Schools.

A native of Swansea he is a past chairman of the South West Wales Industrial Archaeology Society.

When not writing, lecturing, flying or motorcycling he is an active campaigner on behalf of all things Welsh.

By the same author:

A Gazeteer of the Welsh Slate Industry	ISBN 0-86381-196-5
Slate Quarrying at Corris	ISBN 0-86381-279-1
Slate Quarrying in Wales	ISBN 0-86381-319-4
Slate Quarrying in Pembrokeshire	ISBN 0-86381-484-0
The Slate Regions of North & Mid Wales	ISBN 0-86381-552-9

Publisher, Gwasg Carreg Gwalch

Contents

Acknowledgements

I owe a considerable debt to the patient help of the staffs of the National Library of Wales and the Caernarfon, Dolgellau, Anglesey, Aberystwyth, Llangefni, Carmarthen & Haverfordwest Record Offices. Also to the encouragement and advice of amongst others, Dr David Gwyn, Dr G.P. Jones, Griff R. Jones, D. Haydn Lewis, the late Dafydd Price, Dr Dafydd Roberts, Merfyn Williams, Richard M. Williams, and in particular my wife Delphine.

Foreword

The railways of the Slate Industry were as vital then as air travel is to twenty first century man. The development of this fascinating mode of transport justifiably deserves the historical research which the book you are now holding gives it. The Slate Railways of Wales by Alun John Richards presents an overall picture of the subject which some of the more specialised volumes might miss in their concentration on one specific area of research and presentation. This volume is a valuable addition to any enthusiast's or historian's library, who is interested in the areas of Victorian Industrial history and Victorian Industrial Railways, which made Wales a world name in the sphere of the Slate Industry.

The fact that Mr Richards is himself an engineer, with experience of working with the slate industry, will through his professional background bring fresh light on many aspects of this subject.

I am delighted to have been invited to write this foreword and I hope that you will enjoy reading this book as much as Mr Richards has undoubtedly done in researching and preparing it.

Richard Douglas Pennant

Preface

During the latter decades of the 18th century, coal and coal dependent industries grew in size and importance both in south and north-east Wales as well as to a lesser degree in south Pembrokeshire. Outside of these coalfield areas metal mining continued, but major mines such as Parys on Anglesey were becoming worked out and dispersed charcoal furnaces lapsed into obsolescence. Woollen manufacture, traditionally a rural cottage industry, was becoming concentrated into town factories. This left much of Wales increasingly dependent on agriculture, frequently at a subsistence level on sour, undrained soils.

Most of the best land was held by big estates often run as feudal fiefdoms, where tenants were constrained by enclosures and crushed by oppressive rents. In even the most fertile regions the only agricultural surpluses which could be readily marketed were drovable livestock. Upland areas eked an existence by barter, their fragile economies strained by population growth. Thus Wales was divided into two nations, the Industrial Nation, its workers benefiting from finite working hours rewarded by regular and by the standards of the time not ungenerous wages, and the Rural Nation, surviving on pittances.

With the outbreak of war with France in 1793, industry boomed arming and clothing the troops, while the countryside faced rising prices, food shortages and even greater impoverishment. When between 1795 and 1801, four out of seven harvests failed, the Industrial/Rural divide became a chasm, which impended serious political and social consequences.

Fortunately as industrial conurbations flourished, so did their need for slate to roof their factories, warehouses, public buildings and teeming terraces.

Happily it was in some of the most impecunious rural areas of Wales that slate abounded, creating industries on bare hillsides and converting tiny isolated settlements into vibrant communities.

The transport demands of slate caused tramways and railways to be laid to some of the remotest places. The economic benefits of rail connection to hitherto inaccessible locations are obvious but the resultant social inclusion was equally important, enabling a sharing in the progress and prosperity of the Victorian era. Nor must one neglect the direct employment impact. Besides the obvious footplatemen, guards, signalmen, platelayers and engine shed and dray men, which at a major junction could total hundreds, even the smallest station had several staff, and almost every by-road crossing had its keeper.

In addition, without the slate inspired lines, the railways would have largely followed an east-west axis, reinforcing the division of Wales into distinct north, mid and south zones, each an appendage of an English region. At least in part due to slate requirements a comprehensive network emerged enabling persons from almost anywhere in Wales to meet and return within the day, assisting the development of pan-Wales organisations. This promoted a consciousness of Wales as an economic, social and political entity. More importantly railway communications fostered a cultural awareness resulting in the eisteddfodic revival and the flourishing of a Welsh press.

Less obvious, but in the long-term even more important was the effect of railways on education. Children from outlying homes whose teaching might otherwise have been severely circumscribed, could attend British and National or later on, County schools, enabling many to attain eminence in medicine, the law, politics and other professions.

AJR 2001

Spelling

Present day spellings are used for place names e.g. *Porthmadog*. Where they form part of a company title, the original official spelling is normally used e.g. *Festiniog & Blaenau Railway*. Where this original spelling has been formally revised, the revised form is used e.g. *Ffestiniog Railway*, even in an historical context.

Except where a company named its horse drawn or gravity powered line a 'Railway', such lines are referred to as 'Tramways', otherwise the term 'Railway' in the text implies locomotive haulage.

During the mid 19th century, the term Narrow Gauge was applied (often in a pejorative sense) to 4' 8½" track to distinguish it from the 7' 0¼" Broad Gauge. Although the strict modern usage calls for any track of less than Standard Gauge to be called Narrow Gauge, in this book this term applies to gauges of about 2'.

Rolling Stock

The description of rolling stock is outside the scope of this book, but since narrow gauge locomotive tended to be specified to individual requirements, reflecting local needs and circumstances, a brief mention of some is included.

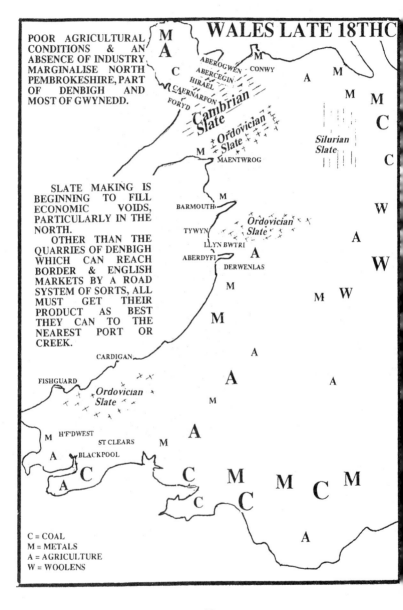

WALES LATE 18THC

POOR AGRICULTURAL CONDITIONS & AN ABSENCE OF INDUSTRY MARGINALISE NORTH PEMBROKESHIRE, PART OF DENBIGH AND MOST OF GWYNEDD.

SLATE MAKING IS BEGINNING TO FILL ECONOMIC VOIDS, PARTICULARLY IN THE NORTH.

OTHER THAN THE QUARRIES OF DENBIGH WHICH CAN REACH BORDER & ENGLISH MARKETS BY A ROAD SYSTEM OF SORTS, ALL MUST GET THEIR PRODUCT AS BEST THEY CAN TO THE NEAREST PORT OR CREEK.

M A

C

ABEROGWEN - CONWY
ABERCEGIN
HIRAEL
CAERNARFON
FORYD

Cambrian Slate

Ordovician Slate

Silurian Slate

M

MAENTWROG

M

BARMOUTH

Ordovician Slate

TYWYN

LLYN BWTRI

ABERDYFI

DERWENLAS

M

M

M W

M

A

W

W

A

W

M

CARDIGAN

A

FISHGUARD

Ordovician Slate

A

A

M

M H'F'DWEST

ST CLEARS

M

A

BLACKPOOL

A

C

C

C

M

M

C

M

C

A

C = COAL
M = METALS
A = AGRICULTURE
W = WOOLENS

1 The Background

'Railed Roads' were late coming to Wales. Although wagonways had been in use in the north of England from at least the early 17th century, it was not until 1697 that Sir Humphrey Mackworth laid one from a colliery to the river at Neath. This line like those which shortly followed it, such as the Mancot and the Latchcroft wagonways which carried coal to the river Dee at Queensferry and Shotton respectively, had wooden wheels and rails. Following the introduction of iron wheels from around 1730, rails were iron sheathed and although such rails remained in use well into the 19th century, from about the 1760s rails were generally of cast iron, by which time tramways were beginning to proliferate in the coal and iron districts of Wales, with their use really taking off at the end of the 18th century.

Although the notion of running vehicles on rails was slow to be adopted in Wales, the propelling of them by steam was not. Trevethick's pioneering 1804 demonstration on the Penydarren tramway led to steam being used on other Welsh coalfield tramways, as celebrated in the mildly ribald 'Crawshay's Engine' song.

Despite this, the 'Railway Mania' which followed the 1830 opening of the Liverpool & Manchester Railway did not spread to Wales. Lines such as the Llanelly and Taf Vale, which opened in 1839 and 1840 respectively, were in every respect full-blown railways, but functioned as 'mechanised colliery tramways' dedicated to carrying coal to a seaport, totally distinct from the sort of 'intercity' network developing in England.

Not that Wales was ignored by English railway speculators, as early as 1834 schemes were being put forward to lay rails across Wales to improve communications with Ireland, which since the Act of Union of 1800 had become increasingly important. So important in fact that in 1836 the Drummond Commission was set up to identify port sites and to survey possible railway routes to them.

Holyhead ought to have been the obvious destination. Connected with London by Telford's road, the harbour had been upgraded in 1821, and five years later the hazards of the Menai ferry had been eliminated by Telford's bridge, enabling it to become the primary port for Ireland. However the Menai road bridge was considered such a feat that to build another bridge capable of carrying speeding locomotives was unthinkable. In fact it was suggested that if trains were ever to venture onto Anglesey, the wagons and carriages would have to be drawn across the Telford bridge by horses.

Therefore ports on the mainland were considered, with Aberystwyth, Fishguard, Newquay and Pembroke being amongst the early suggestions. In 1836 the Great Western Railway backed, Great Welsh Junction Railway, proposed Bangor and also an entirely new harbour at Porth Dinllaen on the north coast of the Llyn peninsular.

Developing a harbour at Porth Dinllaen would have avoided the Menai crossing, but to have followed the Telford road through Snowdonia would have involved daunting engineering and a north coast route would have meant bridging the Conwy and negotiating the towering cliffs at Penmaenmawr. The establishment of 'St. George's Harbour' at Llandudno was proposed to avoid these obstacles, but this would have made the sea voyage unacceptably long. Consequently ways of reaching Porth Dinllaen via Porthmadog and Pwllheli were considered.

One suggested route would have followed the Dee valley from Ruabon to Bala, then having passed north of Dolgellau at high level, would cross the Mawddach at Llanelltyd by a 35 arch viaduct. Maintaining elevation, it would pass behind

Barmouth, follow the coast to Pwllheli, crossing the Glaslyn estuary via the Porthmadog cob, and swing north to Porth Dinllaen. A shorter alternative would have turned north at Bala and ploughed across country to Maentwrog, but this would have called for a long tunnel between the Tryweryn and the Prysor valleys and a steep cable worked incline, from Trawsfynydd down to Maentwrog.

Reaching Barmouth via Newtown, Machynlleth and Tywyn would have called for a crossing of the Mawddach estuary and a long tunnel at Talerddig. This latter would have been avoided by bringing a line in from Shrewsbury to Llanfair Caereinion via the Meifod valley, then along the turnpike (now the A458) to Mallwyd and thence to Machynlleth. The gradients and the tunnelling would have been intimidating, but not as intimidating as a variation on this which would have turned the line north at Mallwyd and hacked across country to Trawsfynydd. More bizarre was an idea to reach Machynlleth not by the Dyfi valley but by turning south a couple of miles short of Mallwyd and driving across country via Cwm Tafolog and Cwm Rhiw Saeson to Llanbrynmair.

Following the Drummond Commission report the rush to obtain Acts became a stampede. Some favoured a northern route, such as the Chester to Ormeshead (Llandudno) Railway, (which had the backing of Lord Mostyn as an outlet for his Wrexham collieries) and the Shrewsbury & Portdinlaen Railway. Others like the Welsh Midland Railway in all its various guises and titles sought multiple coastal destinations, aiming at Aberystwyth, Neath, Swansea and Fishguard. Some were more focused but showed equally arrogant disregard for both economics and topography. These included the Crewe & Aberystwyth Railway and the Gloucester, Aberystwyth and Central Wales Railway and the Manchester & Milford Haven Railway (with famously its 86 directors).

The best founded scheme seemed to be the Great Western backed broad gauge Worcester & Porthdinlaen Railway, an 1845 rehash of the Great Welsh Junction Railway, which would have entered Wales at Llanymynech south of Oswestry and other than some heavy engineering and a tunnel to reach Bala, would have had a relatively easy passage to the coast via the Wnion valley and Dolgellau. Directly this failed to find support, the Great North & South Wales Railway (also broad gauge), sought to incorporate its route, adding branches to Cardigan and Carmarthen via Aberystwyth. This railway aimed to plough through hill and dale and smash through the middle of any town which happened to be in its path. The 19½ mile Llanfihangel yr Arth-Cardigan section had 5 tunnels totalling 3¼ miles. The 66 mile Machynlleth-Carmarthen section would have had 16 tunnels totalling 9¼ miles and would have cut a swathe through the centres of both Aberystwyth and Carmarthen. An alternative scheme on similar routes called itself the East & West Wales Railway.

The 1845 Hawkshaw Gauge Report effectively put a stop to broad gauge ideas in north Wales, although a 7' gauge line was later used at Holyhead harbour, which actually remained in use, steam hauled to 1913.

Indeed, Holyhead still had adherents such as the Trent Valley, Chester & Holyhead Continuation Railway and its rival Trent Valley Continuation & Holyhead Junction Railway. Others, such as the Direct London & Dublin Railway and the North Wales Railway proposed Bangor as the port for Ireland.

Among the crazier notions were the atmospheric railways aiming to minimise tunnelling etc. by using the reputed ability of atmospheric propulsion to deal with gradients steeper than the 1 in 300 considered the maximum for locomotive haulage. The Grand London & Dublin Approximation Railway aimed to reach Bangor via Betws-y-coed and the Nant Ffrancon pass, which apart from anything else, would have called for some 70 or 80 pumping stations along the route. The really most outrageous atmospheric proposal was the London & Holyhead & Dynlleyn Railway, which proposed to reach the two destinations via the Llanberis pass. Instead of using the semi-successful Cleg/Samuda system, it planned to use the outlandish Pilbrow system where the piston in the under-track vacuum tube instead of pulling the train along, operated capstans between the rails which propelled the train via racks. Like the Trent Valley proposals, exactly how it would cross Menai was not made clear.

Eventually in the late 1840s, Robert Stephenson boldly grasped the nettle of both the Conwy and the Menai crossings, enabling the Chester & Holyhead Railway to be built along the north coast. This line became part of the London & North Western Railway, an 1846 amalgamation of the London & Birmingham Railway and the canal sponsored Grand Junction Railway. At the same time the transatlantic orientated South Wales Railway, was laying its Great Western backed broad gauge rails along the south coast.

The purpose of these two railways, like their abortive predecessors, was to connect the manufacturing and commercial centres of England with ports in the west of Wales. Their intention was not to go to Wales, but to go through Wales, any business they could pick up on the way being a gratuitous bonus. Such was the perceived attraction of such trans-Wales routes that even after the C. & H.R. and the S.W.R. had effectively established a duopoly, splendidly-titled proposals continued.

In 1852 the North & South Wales Railway was revived (without the 'Great') and rehashed a year later as the North & South Wales & Worcester. Likewise from 1854 the Manchester & Milford Haven having amalgamated with the gloriously titled Manchester & Birmingham Continuation & Welch Junction Railway was for several years recycled under various elaborate titles almost on an annual basis. Eventually in 1867 a line from Aberystwyth to Carmarthen would carry the simple but highly misleading title of Manchester & Milford Railway.

In the meantime, from mid century numerous companies, many of them locally sponsored, began to run their tracks up, down and across the industrial valleys of the south, while in the north-east, every mine and manufactory would become laced into a densely interlocking pattern of lines.

By this time the effects of the Joint Stock Companies Acts of 1855-56 were being felt. Railway capital was no longer coming just from the very rich or the very foolish, limited liability was attracting local landowners, traders and professional men. These more sanguine investors tended only to part with their cash, where there were prospects of sound returns.

Even at this time, with the Railway Age a quarter of a century old, and the Act of 1844 enforcing 'penny a mile' travel, the potential of passenger traffic was not fully appreciated. It may have been that it was thought that the number of persons prepared to be crammed into open wagons was limited, or perhaps that 'Parliamentary' travellers were not the class of client a railway would wish to encourage. Despite the fact that a passenger carriage had a potential revenue of 4/- (20p) per mile as against perhaps 10d (4.16p) for a bulk wagon, bulk freight was seen as the profit generator, which in Wales outside of the coalfields meant slate.

Both the 1860 West Midlands, Shrewsbury and Welsh Coast Railway (re-submitted five years later without the 'West') and the 1864 Potteries, Shrewsbury and North Wales Railway also sought to cross Wales. Although both did have half an eye on Porth Dinllaen, their main objective was slate and other minerals. It is interesting that these lines sought to bring Shrewsbury into the Welsh railway ambit, suggesting an intention to re-establish that town's long standing function as the 'wool capital' of mid Wales. The W.M.S. & W.C. was never built and only a few miles of the 'Potts' was laid (which later would form part of the Shropshire & Montgomeryshire Light Railway), but two local initiatives did succeed.

In the mid 1850s the Shrewsbury & Aberystwyth and the Montgomeryshire Railways were competing to build a line through mid Wales to Aberystwyth. In 1859 the good citizens of Llanidloes fearing that the S. & A. and the M.R.'s squabbles would leave their town marginalised, opened their own railway. This Llanidloes & Newtown Railway was the first indigenous Welsh standard gauge steam railway outside of the coalfields. Having united these two important woollen centres and linked into the national network via the Oswestry & Newtown Railway, rails had by the mid 1860s, reached right across Wales to the coast and were thrusting north towards the slate riches of Gwynedd. Concurrently the similarly locally inspired Ruabon-Dolgellau route was pursuing the same objectives.

During the 1860s almost 700 miles of line were completed, reaching the majority of Welsh towns. Without the lure of slate much of this mileage as well as a number of lines opened in north-west Wales during the ensuing decades would not have been built. This would have left that, and indeed other regions, isolated and unable to share the benefits of rail connection which revolutionised life in 19th century Britain.

The social and economic benefits of the railways were indeed immense. Food became cheaper and more varied, since the cost of transporting it overland fell from at least 2/- (10p) per ton/mile to perhaps 4d (1.7p). Village shops were able to stock mass produced domestic wares and textiles. The per mile cost of moving coal overland fell from 1/- (5p) per ton or about 10% of pithead price, to as little as 1d (0.4p).

Agriculture became more competitive with the price of

19

lime, a key item on the prevalent acidic soils, falling by up to three-quarters. Produce could be readily dispatched to distant cities, and cattle no longer reached the English conurbations emaciated from weeks on the hoof. Slate-inspired lines enabled woollen manufacture, metal mining and stone quarrying to thrive in isolated locations. In addition several provided the sole means of access to remote and roadless valleys.

The need to transport slate overland obviously predates steam trains, indeed it much predates wheels running on rails and undoubtedly predates the wheels themselves. Slate's transport requirements were exacting since slate is usually found in inaccessible places and, unlike other minerals, is converted into a relatively fragile end product at or near the point of extraction.

At its late 19th century peak the Welsh slate industry grossed, in today's values, some £100,000,000 in units having up to three and four figure payrolls, directly and indirectly providing employment which approached 30,000. Scarcely a century earlier the winning and working of slate had been carried out by a few hundred men working as individuals or in small partnerships. These early diggings were most prolific in north Caernarfonshire, rather less so in north and south Meirionnydd, with some activity in Denbighshire, Montgomeryshire and north Pembrokeshire.

In these slate regions, the paucity of population, few of whom could afforded to use the product anyway, meant that the overwhelming majority of output had to reach distant markets, mainly by sea.

From at least the 13th century, slate quarried from Cefn Ddu (SH555604) and Cilgwyn (SH500540) was being regularly shipped at Caernarfon and at Foryd (SH458592) respectively. (This little creek should not be confused with the much larger Foryd which was the port for Rhyl.) By the 14th century slate won at Cae Braich-y-cafn near what is now Bethesda, was being shipped at Aberogwen (SH612721) and Abercegin (SH593726). From at least the 16th century slate sourced near the shores of Llyn Padarn was being shipped at Hirael Quay (SH586728). Slate from Aberllefenni was being loaded at Derwenlas (SN719991) on the Dyfi at least a century earlier and shipments of 'Tiling Stones' from Newport (Pembs) may have occurred even before that.

During the 17th century, increases in slate shipments brought about a growth in Welsh shipping and at the same time the slate quarries of Denbighshire expanded an overland trade with towns such as Wrexham, Chester and Shrewsbury.

By the early 18th century, the development of slate working was well under way, gathering pace during that century, with shipments being made at Trefriw on the Conwy, at Maentwrog on the Dwyryd as well as at Aberdyfi, Barmouth and at numerous rivers, creeks and inlets around the coast. By the mid 1700s with Dublin the fastest growing city in Europe, the Cefn Ddu and Cilgwyn quarries were building up an important Irish trade. This was more than matched by the expansion of the Cae Braich-y-cafn and the Padarn quarries who were meeting an increasing demand from the booming textile towns of the north of England, shipping to them via Chester and Liverpool. In addition trade was growing with London and with continental ports, out of which grew a substantial industry, building and operating sailing ships. The use of sailing ships continued well into the steamship era, partly because they could operate in tiny harbours without coaling facilities, but also because the time needed for the safe stowage of slate cargoes was unpopular with steamship owners seeking quick turnarounds.

Whilst slate was found in limited quantities on the coast of north Pembrokeshire and at Llaneilian on Anglesey, better and more abundant rock tended to occur some distance from navigable water. Although those distances were generally only a few miles, carriage was difficult and costly. Paradoxically it was the inland quarries of Denbighshire that were in some ways best placed to reach their markets. Although they had to rely on lumbering carts, they were close to Wrexham which in the mid 18th century was the largest population centre in Wales. Chester, Shrewsbury, and the English midlands were also readily accessible thanks to the good roads of the Cheshire plain.

Not so in the upland north-west. Roads were few and often impassable in winter, some villages had scarcely ever seen a wheeled vehicle. Such roads as existed were parish roads, theoretically maintained by the parishioners, an obligation which even where enforced, could often be discharged by a token payment. A few roads were constructed by large landowners but these were understandably sited solely for the convenience of their estates. When turnpike roads belatedly came to the north and the west, they were few, they were usually routed to suit long-distance through traffic and their tolls were onerous.

Pack animals, tended by young women, were the commonest means of carrying slate for shipment. In fact the traditional unit of sale, the Cant Mawr (Big Hundred) of 128 slates represented the nominal capacity of a pair of horse or mule panniers. The Padarn quarries could make part of their journey by boat along Llyn Padarn, but at some of the small diggings slates had to be carried on the backs of the men who had produced them, and in some cases on those of their wives and older children. Where cartage was possible the state of the roads meant that an appreciable proportion of slates arrived broken and unusable. It was not exceptional for the cost of carrying output to a shipping point to exceed the cost of production.

Neither the parishes nor the landlords had any incentive to improve roads to suit the convenience of the slate diggers. At the same time the scale of quarrying was too small and the customary annual Take Note tenure too short, to warrant the quarrymen making road improvements.

It was in the penultimate decade of the 18th century that an event occurred, which would have a dramatic impact on slate quarrying and its transport.

Richard Pennant, the son of a wealthy Liverpool merchant had acquired by marriage a share in the Penrhyn estate which included a tract of land extending from the coast near Bangor up the Ogwen valley including the slate diggings on Cae Braich-y-cafn. He had immediately put his diggers on formal leases and had used his Liverpool connections to appoint an agent to assist them to sell into booming south Lancashire.

Having come into sole ownership of the estate in 1782, he cancelled the leases and set about quarrying on his own account forming what would become Penrhyn quarry at SH620650. Now for the first time slate was being produced on an industrial basis, backed by a wealthy freeholder who also owned the sea shore and the intervening land.

In the early 1790s Pennant, by now ennobled by inheritance as Lord Penrhyn, was employing at least 400 men and had established Port Penrhyn at Abercegin, connected to his quarry by improved roads.

In the meantime events at the Padarn quarries which were on the Faenol Estate were following a similar course. In 1787, the owner Thomas Assheton-Smith, whilst not initially involving himself directly in quarrying, granted a lease to the Dinorwig Slate Company to consolidate the diggings into one unit at SH595603. He also encouraged the building of roads and by 1793 had begun the development of Port Dinorwig at Y Felinheli (SH525679).

Thus by the closing years of the 18th century road improvements had enabled Penrhyn quarry to achieve a dominance which it retains to the present day and had set

Dinorwig quarry on the path to an almost equal ascendancy which lasted until 1969.

However, although pack animals had been superseded by carts at both these quarries, their transport was still far from satisfactory. The Penrhyn wagons although of nominal two ton capacity reputedly could only carry one ton or even less in winter. Dinorwig's roads were eventually marginally better than Penrhyn's, but both quarries suffered from the intransigence of the farmers who supplied the horses and drivers. Transport shortcomings were exacerbated in the 1790s by steep increases in feed costs and by the tax on horses levied both to raise revenue and to encourage their owners to release them for army service. Casting about for a solution, Penrhyn tried using oxen, a commonplace draught animal on smaller farms, but these proved unsatisfactory.

Hence at the start of the 19th century, the arrangements for moving slate to market called for drastic revision.

This broadly took place in four overlapping phases.

1801 on   The two major quarries lay private tramways to dedicated private ports. This improves competitiveness, promotes expansion and encourages ancillary and support activities at the ports and along routes. No public use, hence no direct public benefits and competing quarries are marginalised.

1828 on   In emulation of the above, two public, commercial tramways to existing ports, enable groups of quarries in two areas to collectively form another two major sources. Considerable direct benefits especially from carriage of food and fuel.

1852 on   Standard gauge steam lines laid down for other purposes are able to intercept pre-existing major tramways, widening slate market by facilitating distribution to inland destinations. Several minor tramways laid, mainly to shipping points.

1860 on   Proliferation of standard gauge steam railways, many competing for slate traffic. At the same time numerous tramways and narrow gauge steam railways and standard gauge branches built, increasingly as feeders to main lines rather than to ports. These open up second rank and minor slate areas. Widespread benefits accrue, including passenger travel.

By 1872 over 90% of Welsh slate output had railed access to the national railways. Ten years later slate-related railway construction was effectively complete, and slate-related shipping and shipbuilding had commenced a rundown, which was almost total by WW1.

On the face of it this decline should have happened in the 1850s, but initially rail charges were too high to compete with shipping to coastal destinations and even places well inland could often be economically reached via a canal by shipping to an appropriate English seaport. In fact some quarries in north-east Wales could directly access the English waterways network via the Llangollen or the Montgomeryshire canals. Added to which, up to the late 1870s the expansion in the slate industry was so great that seemingly unlimited tonnages could be sent by rail without encroaching on the ports' traffic.

Inexorably the supplanting of wooden sailing ships by iron steam ships, ended shipbuilding at the small creeks and harbours, and the increasing size of vessels limited the scope of the creeks and harbours themselves. In addition rail charges gradually became more competitive and customers grew impatient with the delays and breakages implicit in quayside loading and unloading. This speeded the end of local shipping, a process that would eventually be completed by pallets and containers.

Some coastal shipping managed to survive into the 1960s,

ironically the same decade that saw the effective obliteration of rail freight, both victims of the onslaught of road haulage.

By a curious coincidence the great railway era when few dwellings were more than 5 miles from a station and only two towns, St Davids and Beaumaris were not rail-connected, almost exactly coincided with the prime of the slate industry. This is fitting since the abundance of lines in Wales' remoter districts with for instance, Meirionnydd having more than 3 miles of rail per 1000 inhabitants against a UK average of less than ¾ mile, was substantially due to the demands of that industry.

2 Up to 1830. The First Rails

The Penrhyn, Dinorwig and Nantlle Tramroads

In the 1790s war-time constraints on building and the disruption of coastal trade by French warships put the expanding demand for slate sharply into reverse.

Far from being dismayed at his quarry's sales being more than halved, Lord Penrhyn saw the recession as an opportunity to build a transport link to the port which would make more efficient use of the increasingly expensive horses and which would prepare for the upsurge which he believed would come with the war's end. It would also relieve distress by providing jobs for laid-off workers and discourage men from seeking jobs in the then booming metallurgical industries at Greenfield, Bersham, etc.

The outcome was the pioneering, 6¼ mile **Penrhyn Railroad**. Whilst it is impossible to exaggerate the importance of this line, the earliest known railed line dedicated to the carrying of slate, it was not the first tramway to be built on Penrhyn land, which was the short Llandegai Flint Mill Tramway. The need for this line arose because Penrhyn's slate agent Samuel Worthington, having an interest in a pottery at Liverpool, built a kiln at Port Penrhyn to calcine flint, using coal from Deeside, both being brought in on the slate vessels as return loads. He also built a mill to grind the calcined material at SH600707, where it could be powered by a leat from the river Ogwen. The out-turn was returned to the port in barrels as slurry for shipment to Liverpool.

In 1798 the port and the mill were connected by a tramway, which consisted of a run of about ¾ mile through Llandygái with inclines down at each end. Shortly afterwards a second mill was established worked from the tailrace of the first to saw timber for writing slate frames.

This line was not immediately adopted as a prototype for a quarry transport route, since although running a wagon on rails could multiply a horse's effort by up to a factor of 10, pulling a canal barge the factor was nearer 50. Accordingly Thomas Dadford, then one of the leading canal and tramway engineers, was commissioned to make a survey for a canal from the quarry to Port Penrhyn. As locks could not cope with a fall of almost 600' in 6 miles, barges would have had to be laboriously dragged on inclines in up to eight places. In addition, the icy winters around the turn of the century had underlined the problems caused by the freezing of canals in elevated locations.

Wisely, it was decided to take the tramway option, for which Dadford also produced plans. A gauge of 4' or so was current iron and coal practice, a dimension which owed more to the size and capabilities of a horse rather than the anecdotal spacing of Roman chariot wheels, but wagons of this gauge could not be conveniently manhandled within the confines of a quarry. Dadford suggested a gauge of 5' 2", presumably with the intention of carrying small quarry wagons pic-a-back. He conformed to the fashion of the time in specifying 'L' section tram plates and narrow wagon wheels, rather than the then less popular edge rails and flanged wheels, but to maintain acceptable gradients inclines would still be required. The self-acting drum incline, which became the industry standard, had been patented by a Michael Meinzies in 1750 but until wire ropes became available in the mid century, pitch lengths were limited. Therefore chains, which were just coming into widespread use following their recent adoption by the Navy, were specified. Owing to their weight, chains had to be endless, the resulting tail-rope preserving the self-action. Instead of a drum, there were vertical line-side sheaves at the head and foot of the inclines, presumably based on the horse-whim powered arrangements on the flint mill line.

When Penrhyn agent Benjamin Wyatt, took over the

building of the line, he adopted a gauge of 24½" (over rail centres). Such a gauge minimised construction costs, was suitable for use within the quarry, gave a handy size of wagon for working the inclines and was probably already in use on the flint mill line. Less well advised was his choice of track. He did not like tram plates since to his mind such track could not be properly 'gravelled'. Nor did he like stone blocks which could not accurately maintain gauge. Accordingly he specified edge rails raised well up on 'sills' (integral chair/sleepers) kinked to lay well below ballast level where they could not obstruct the horses. So far so good but he specified a double-flanged wheel layout which Dadford had tried in south Wales but had abandoned in favour of the Outram L-plate. Wyatt's version had oval section rail on which ran wheels with a concave rim of slightly greater radius than the upper surface of the rail thus offering almost point contact, – until wear having made the radii identical, the wheels jammed on the rails! Curiously he used wheels fixed to the axle, unnecessary with what was effectively a double-flanged layout, this was also a source of jamming due to distortion and/or manufacturing tolerance failing to keep the rails exactly to gauge. In addition at 14" diameter the wheels were smaller than would have been ideal.

With these shortcomings still unforeseen, the Penrhyn Railroad commenced work on 25th June 1801, being officially opened on 1st July 1801 by Lord Penrhyn (followed by the obligatory 'Cold Collation' at the port). It started at Coed y Parc (SH615663) which later became the engineering and maintenance centre for the quarry. From there the line ran for about a mile to the Cilgeraint incline which dropped it 63'. A further 1½ miles took it to the Dinas incline dropping it 58'. After almost another 3 miles, having joined the flint mill tramway at Llandygái it dropped a further 102' on the Marchogion incline (which it shared with the flint line) and thence about ¾ mile to the port. On all the inclines wagons were crewled three at a time. The non-incline sections had an almost constant fall of about 1 in 100, assisting the loaded journeys without impeding the return of empties, which together with the well separated inclines, gave it an ideal layout. It was claimed that even with the delays of crewling wagons on the inclines, six trains of up to 24 wagons, each carrying up to a ton, drawn by 2 or 3 horses, could pass each way daily giving a theoretical capacity of some 40,000 tons per annum, way over the foreseeable output of the quarry. A near contemporary account stated that only 16 horses were required to replace 400 drawing carts. This is possibly an exaggeration, but nevertheless a dramatic reduction in both horse and man power was achieved.

The line's opening coincided with a recovery in trade, and gave Penrhyn quarry a uniquely cheap and reliable route to the sea. Besides this, the quarry's increasing need for timber and other supplies could form return loads. In due course as mechanisation of the quarry developed, the ability to bring in engineering materials and coal would become vital.

A year after the tramway opened a slate sawing mill was established at Port Penrhyn, which set the port on the way to being an industrial site in its own right, with independent slate merchant/processors such as Dixon & Co. setting up there.

The line's considerable overcapacity proved fortunate as the idiosyncratic rails proved unsatisfactory, the high friction causing delays when the wheels became even slightly worn. Substantial track replacement was carried out by 1807 and probably again in 1821 when part of the route at Llandygái was re-aligned enabling the new turnpike to be underpassed eliminating the level crossing. The old rails and their iron sleepers were replaced by conventional edge rails and wooden sleepers on 1' 10¾" gauge. Later the vertical drums and chains of the inclines were replaced by conventional horizontal drums and ropes.

In spite of the problems, it has been estimated that the line enabled a ton of slate to reach the port at a cost of 1/- (5p) against a cost of 5/- (25p) by cart. An appreciable saving on a product worth little more than a pound or so per ton and enough to recover the cost of construction in two or three years.

None of this was any use whatsoever to the diggers operating on adjacent non-Penrhyn land. They still had to cart to the rather sketchy facilities at Aberogwen, where Lord Penrhyn allowed them to load ship but would not permit slates to be stacked there to await shipment.

This line enabled the Penrhyn dynasty to assert their authority over the whole industry. Whatever may be said about them as employers, their early leadership and foresight substantially contributed to Welsh slate's world dominance.

In the meantime, Dinorwig had suffered less loss of trade from the effects of the war, but whilst its output was still modest compared with Penrhyn, it was by far the second largest quarry in Wales.

Although by 1800 the use of pack animals to carry to Penisa'r-waun (SH557640) for loading onto carts had largely been replaced by sledging down to Llyn Peris and boating along Llyn Padarn to Cwm-y-glo (SH559623), Dinorwig's transport remained difficult and costly. However, unlike Penrhyn, the landlord Thomas Assheton-Smith was not directly involved so presumably was reluctant to bank-roll a railed route.

In 1809 the original Dinorwig company was reformed with landlord Thomas Assheton-Smith taking a direct interest. This presumably should have obviated any funding obstacles to the building of a tramway, yet even though rails were increasingly used within the quarry, including inclines down to the lakeside, they do not seem to have been seriously considered as a means of taking product to Port Dinorwig. As late as 1812 a relatively expensive road was built, running through what would become the present village of Deiniolen.

It was only in 1821 when Assheton-Smith took sole possession of the quarry, that a rail link was decided on. Grandly named the **Dinorwig Railway**, it was completed in 1824.

In spite of Penrhyn's double-flanged wheels having proved a failure they were copied and to the same 24½" gauge, the error being compounded by the use of slate sleepers instead of cast-iron sleepers which were probably the one redeeming feature of the original Penrhyn track.

At just over 7 miles it was a little longer than the Penrhyn Tramway, but its fall of 1000' was nearly twice as great. Almost half this drop was made a mile from the start at the two tandem pitches of the Cwm incline, which having only a constricted swan-neck between them, were difficult to work. Four miles beyond was the Garth incline with a 200' drop, followed by a final run of ¾ mile to Port Dinorwig along the route of the 1812 road access to the port, crossing the Bangor-Caernarfon turnpike by an underpass. Since, unlike the Penrhyn, the horses were quarry owned rather than belonging to contractors, there was need for stables. There was one at the foot of the Cwm inclines, another at the head of the Garth incline and a third at Efail Castell (SH565655) half way between, with additional stabling at the quarry and the port.

Unlike the Penrhyn with its steady 1 in 100 fall, the first section built on the pre-existing road to the Cwm incline was almost level. The average fall of the 4 mile haul was an acceptable 1 in 80, but this was far from constant and the final section to the port was a steep 1 in 50. To compound matters, in places some of the earthworks were barely adequate for the boggy ground, leading to track settlement. Much more serious was the fact that although it passed conveniently close to the small Allt Ddu and Chwarel Fawr workings, much of the main quarry extraction was taking place at a lower level.

The uphaulage to reach the line and its various operating and maintenance difficulties, meant that its benefit to Dinorwig's costs and efficiency was limited. This together with its short life, ranks it rather low in importance on any list of quarry-inspired railed routes. However, it did establish Deiniolen as a slate manufacturing centre, with ultimately four writing-slate factories. Such writing slate or enamelling factories were frequently sited in towns or villages to offer employment to elderly or mildly unfit men and also to women whose presence on a quarry site was regarded as a harbinger of bad luck.

So at the end of the first quarter of the 19th century, in two of the three then main slate regions of Wales a dominant quarry had a dedicated port, reached by private railways whose wagons as it were, were hitched to the star of the explosive expansion of the Lancashire cotton towns.

In the third region, where the ancient Cilgwyn diggings had spread through the Nantlle valley, very different conditions prevailed. The ground was in the hands of at least three separate landowners each letting out numerous patches some of which were very small. Thus there was no dominant 'superquarry' run by a long-pocketed proprietor, let alone one owning both the seaboard and the intervening land, who could readily establish a port and lay down roads or rails.

Furthermore the Cilgwyn/Nantlle area trading mainly with Ireland was missing out on the textile-driven north of England bonanza. Even so, the numerous quarries' combined output had overwhelmed the shipment facilities at Foryd, hence the Caernarfon slate quays which from the early 1800s had been developed on reclaimed land in front of the castle, were increasingly used for dispatching their product. The turnpike running north from Penygroes eased the journey, but its tolls were burdensome. Although the slight premium which Nantlle slate could command over Penrhyn product might compensate for Nantlle's more difficult conditions and smaller scale of working, cartage costs threatened to make their operations uneconomic.

Aware of the economies which the tramway had brought Penrhyn, the proprietors of the largest quarries, Cilgwyn (SH500540), Pen y Bryn (SH502536), Tal y Sarn (SH496534) and Hafod Las (SH489540), joined to consider building a rail line on a collective basis. It was only when the opening of the Dinorwig line concentrated their minds, that a company was formed and a Parliamentary Bill obtained to construct the **Nantlle Railway** as the first public railway in north Wales.

Although mileage would have been halved by running directly to the coast, the availability of ready made shipment facilities at Caernarfon, recently improved by the Marquis of Anglesey partly to create jobs for ex-soldiers who had fought under him at Waterloo, outweighed the extra mileage. With the emergence of dedicated slate ports such as Penrhyn and Dinorwig threatening to marginalise existing harbours, the burgesses of Caernarfon must have been greatly relieved at that decision.

Gradients would be moderate but for the first mile or so they would be against the load, limiting freights to 4 tons per horse, half of what one could draw on a level track, and a third of what could be pulled on the constantly falling Penrhyn line. Thus although minimal civil work with no inclines gave little constructional advantage to a narrow gauge, the adverse gradient made a gauge of 4' or more undesirable. In the event, as a compromise the Flintshire colliery gauge of 3' 6" was chosen, a gauge which may have already been in use in Pen y Bryn quarry.

Although plateways were now going out of fashion, it was planned to lay this type of track, possibly with a view to road carts being able to use it, a well known but rarely used advantage of plateways. Although the plates were bought, they were sold off unused and chaired fish-belly edge rails made to Birkenshaw's 1820 patent were laid. Whilst more satisfactory than the Penrhyn and Dinorwig bar rails, they too had eventually to be replaced by flat-bottom rail.

This gauge worked well since the outboard-wheeled wagons were comparatively small-bodied, limiting their loads to about 2 tons, which was not excessive for manhandling within the quarries. Problems did arise when quarries began to use locomotives which practicality and availability limited to about 2' gauge. Then internal lines had to be re-laid to 2' with only the dispatch lines remaining as 3' 6". Internally-used block and rubbish wagons being either 2' gauge, or having loose, double flanged wheels suitable for either gauge. Later, even where locomotives were not used, 2' became widely used within the quarries since wagons, pointwork, etc. were freely obtainable second-hand.

Just over 9 miles long and opened in 1828, the line started at Cloddfa'r Lôn quarry which became part of Pen y Bryn (the extension to Pen yr Orsedd [SH510538] being a later addition). Running west, it passed through some short cut and cover tunnels to Talysarn and on to Penygroes. There it turned north for Caernarfon crossing the Gwyrfai by a stone bridge at Bontnewydd. Just short of Caernarfon it pierced the Coed Helen bluff by a deep cutting and a 22 yard tunnel, finally crossing the Seiont by an iron bridge to run alongside the river to the Slate Quays.

The Nantlle was operated as a 'Rail Turnpike', users providing their own wagons and horses and paying tolls at gates. Tolls were initially 6d (2.5p) per ton mile, which on top of the actual haulage cost, still left the Nantlle quarries seriously disadvantaged as compared with Penrhyn and Dinorwig, but this was still less than half of what carting to Caernarfon had been costing, by toll road. It served most of the quarries on the north side of the valley which were connected to it by short branches or inclines. It being extended to its final terminus at Pen yr Orsedd quarry in the 1860s.

Most of the quarries on the south side of the valley were small, family affairs with limited outputs, with a short and easy cartage to Talysarn. From the 1850s some were served by a branch, extravagantly named the **Carnarvonshire Slate Quarries Railway**. This ran from Fronheulog quarry (SH489517) to join the main line at Pant Ddu between Talysarn and Penygroes. Tan yr Allt quarry (SH491523) reached it via Fronheulog and others may also have used it.

The Nantlle Railway, secured Dyffryn Nantlle's place, at least for a time, as the third largest Welsh slate region. Additionally, it established Caernarfon as a major port and manufacturing centre for slate products and for support and engineering activities.

A further valuable function was the carriage of coal as a return load, since with a dearth of water, the Nantlle pit workings were highly steam dependent for pumping and uphaulage and later, sawing. In fact Cloddfa'r Coed quarry (SH493532) had been in 1807 a pioneer in the use of steam for pumping.

The tramway also generated an on-route writing slate factory at Groeslon. Later trading as Inigo Jones it diversified into enamelled work, although due to the unsuitability of Nantlle slate for this purpose, it later used slate brought in from southern Meirionnydd. Its present day reputation for fine slab work continues to be chiefly based on material from the same area.

As a public line it carried general supplies, not least of which was coal for use in houses, bakeries and public ovens, helping Penygroes and Talysarn, to develop as significant and self supporting communities. In fact the ability to carry coal, often under quarry sponsorship, to remote settlements was one of the most tangible public benefits of slate tramways and railways.

The line also carried product from the Drws y Coed copper mines, thus providing the first example of a slate railway assisting the competitiveness, and indeed the survival of, another industry. In fact, Drws y Coed long outlasted most other Welsh metal mines, continuing to load at Talysarn (product reaching there by steam lorry), into the 20th century.

Although it would be almost thirty years before passengers were regularly carried, casual passenger use was made from the start, almost certainly in ordinary wagons. Although the carrying of passengers by rail was not unknown, the Swansea & Mumbles Railway, for instance having done so in 1807, rails were still regarded as carriers of goods and of the moneyed gentry and would remain so until Gladstone's 'Parliamentary trains' brought mass travel in the 1840s.

However that and all that it implied was in the future. For the time being the Nantlle Railway was the only railed line in north Wales to bring direct benefits to society.

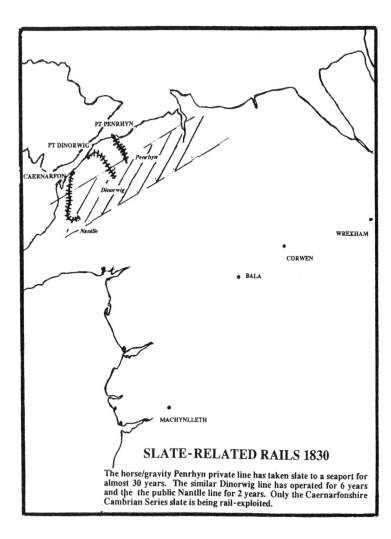

PT PENRHYN

PT DINORWIG

Penrhyn

CAERNARFON

Dinorwig

Nantlle

WREXHAM

CORWEN

BALA

MACHYNLLETH

SLATE-RELATED RAILS 1830

The horse/gravity Penrhyn private line has taken slate to a seaport for almost 30 years. The similar Dinorwig line has operated for 6 years and the the public Nantlle line for 2 years. Only the Caernarfonshire Cambrian Series slate is being rail-exploited.

3 1830-1850. Significant Stirrings

The Ffestiniog and the Padarn

Parallel with the growth of slate working in north Caernarfonshire, things were astir at Blaenau Ffestiniog. Around 1760 Methusalem Jones, an ex-Cilgwyn digger, had formed a partnership to work the bleak and barren hillside at Diffwys (SH712463), starting not only the first substantial slate working in the region, but also probably the first in Wales to have a permanently employed workforce. This quarry was taken over by Turner and the Casson brothers in 1800 and within a few years its output whilst small compared with Penrhyn and Dinorwig, was nevertheless the third largest in Wales. By 1830 its tonnage had almost been eclipsed by Lord Newborough's re-opened Bowydd quarry (SH708462), but by this time both had been overtaken by the Welsh Slate Company's quarry (SH693473), which would soon account for half the Blaenau output. This quarry had been developed by Samuel Holland in 1818 who sold it to the W.S.C.'s predecessors, the Welsh Slate, Copper & Lead Mining Company in 1825, leaving him free to start again at SH690466. In 1833, in between Holland and the W.S.C., Nathaniel Mathew would open up yet another working at SH694470.

These and other smaller Blaenau quarries shipped into two-man boats on the Dwyryd below Maentwrog, which transferred their six ton loads to larger vessels at sea off Ynys y Cyngar, west of Borth-y-gest. Although trans-shipment was eased when Porthmadog harbour opened in 1824, increasing tonnages put a premium on wharfage on the Dwyryd as well as straining the capabilities of the fleet of highly tide-dependent boats.

Formidable though the water part of the journey was, it was easy compared with the difficulties of reaching

Maentwrog. Originally this meant using pack animals the whole way. When the turnpike was built down from Llan Ffestiniog, it could be reached by the parish road from Congl y Wal (SH705444) which in turn could be reached by an indifferent track up a steep gradient from Pont Frongoch (SH703454). Diffwys, in 1801 built their own road to Congl y Wal which gave them a comparatively easy, all downhill route, which was extended in the late 1820s to Rhydysarn (SH690421). Lord Newborough having built a road of sorts from his Bowydd quarry to Pont Frongoch c. 1803, could just about manage to cart, but Holland had to use pack animals to reach Pont Frongoch until 1821 when he built a rudimentary road, which he subsequently shared with the W.S.C. and Mathew. Manod (SH725452) in 1804 built a magnificent and costly road which, partly using pre-existing farm tracks, reached the turnpike near Llan Ffestiniog. The diggings to the east of Mynydd Manod could theoretically reach Llan Ffestiniog down Cwm Teigl, but this was such a scramble that some output was carted down Cwm Machno all the way to the river Conwy at Trefriw.

The road improvements did little to ameliorate the shortage of farmers prepared to provide horses, particularly at harvest times. Nor did it dull the farmers' appreciation of the value of their services, so that typically a quarter or more of a quarry's outgoings were payments for cartage.

Thus by 1830, in territory even more rugged than at Penrhyn or Dinorwig and with land and quarry ownership as diverse as at Nantlle, the five big and several smaller quarries faced serious transport problems. That these problems were not already even worse was due to the Slate Tax, an impost on coastal shipments which had been levied since the 1790s notionally to pay for royal Navy escorts. Being collected on a headport to headport basis it impinged heavily on Welsh quarries, many of whose major markets were Liverpool, Manchester and the cotton towns. These could be reached by entering the canal system at Preston.

Since the up-and-coming north Lancashire quarries shipped at Ulverston, which was within the headport of Preston, theoretically no coastal voyage was involved and therefore no duty was payable. Now fifteen years after Waterloo this wartime tax was still in force.

During the brief trade upsurge at the end of the war, there had been talk of laying rails to run from Bowydd quarry down Cwm Bowydd to Rhydysarn where it would split into two to directly serve the slate wharves on either side of the Dwyryd. While trade was slack around 1820, interest in rails lapsed but when business improved in 1824, fresh ideas were mooted, with the new harbour at Porthmadog rather than the Dwyryd quays as their destination. The first, the original Festiniog Railway (Festiniog, Penrhyndeudraeth & Tanygarth Railway) would have run almost due south from Blaenau and dropped the 700' to the floor of the Dwyryd valley at Dol y Moch (SH682418) by three inclines. It would have run along the north bank of the Dwyryd to serve Holland's and Lord Newborough's wharves and made an end-on junction with the eastern end of the Porthmadog Cob tramway. Presumably it would have been of 3' gauge to match that of the tramway laid by William Madocks c. 1808, to assist in the building of the Cob to reclaim land in the Traeth Mawr estuary, and to be part of a coach route to Porth Dinllaen, then being canvassed as a packet station for Ireland, with Tremadog as a staging town. Quite fortuitously the Cob generated conditions suitable for the establishment of Porthmadog harbour. When the Cob was completed in 1811 the tramway had been lifted only to be hastily relaid the following year to repair a breach, after which it was left in situ.

In 1825 the Festiniog & Portmadoc Railway was surveyed which would have curved around Moelwyn Mawr, dropping down through Rhyd by three inclines and on to Penrhyndeudraeth by a further incline, and from there follow the route eventually adopted by the Ffestiniog

Railway. Like the eventual F.R., it was to have two branches, one to Holland's and one to Bowydd and Diffwys.

The same year the powerful financier Nathan Mayer Rothschild whose Royal Cambrian Company, was seeking slate and copper on the Moelwyns, insisted that any line start at his workings and drop by a series of inclines down to the Glaslyn flood plain, running to Porthmadog on a similar route later taken by the Croesor tramway. Rothschild suggested that the Blaenau quarrymen could uphaul their output the 1000' to the start of his tramway. Since this would cost up to 15/- (75p) per ton against the 12/6 (62.5p) the whole journey was now costing, this was unhelpful. Fortunately Rothschild removed himself from the scene the following year and with trade flat, the rail proposals lapsed. In 1831, largely through the efforts of Foreign Secretary Lord Palmerston, Chairman of the Welsh Slate Company, the Slate Tax was repealed. This started the unbridled expansion of the Welsh slate industry, which would almost double Blaenau's output within six years, bringing an immediate urgency to the solving of its transport difficulties.

Even more owners than at Nantlle were involved and unlike the neighbourliness which has always characterised that area, the Blaenau proprietors tended to be more individualistic. They included the London based directors of the influential but cash-strapped Welsh Slate Company, Lord Newborough and incomer entrepreneurs such as Turner, the Cassons and Samuel Holland. Holland being the most energetic and having moneyed family connections, was the natural leader and it was substantially through his bringing in businessman Henry Archer that the **Ffestiniog Railway** was built. Much of the capital was raised by Archer in his native Dublin, showing the importance of Ireland to the British economy at that time.

Support was not universal. Obviously the carters and boatmen objected and the Turnpike Trust was unenthusiastic at the prospect of their burgeoning revenues virtually vanishing, likewise Diffwys who had found the tolls they were charging on their road were becoming a nice little earner. In addition some landowners such as W.G. Oakeley were obstructive.

Despite the objections and lack of unanimity James Spooner was engaged as engineer and although primarily modelled on the Nantlle line, due to the F.R.'s more demanding topography a gauge of a nominal 2' (later 1' 11½") was chosen. By this time edge rails were firmly back in favour so there was no question of using tramplates.

The main terminus was at Dinas, handy for most of the quarries, with the Duffws branch (as the F.R. spelt it!) from the town joining at the Glan y Pwll junction.

The route taken was the obvious one, picking up the Dwyryd valley as directly as practicable and descending in as constant a gradient as possible to Porthmadog. When the line opened in 1835 it was not possible to maintain an uninterrupted downgrade due to the rising ground at the southern end of Llyn Tanygrisiau. This was ascended by an incline, powered by a 24' x 3' water-wheel, the Nant Ystradau being dammed to supply it. The descent the other side was by a conventional self acting incline.

In 1842 the inclines were by-passed by the 730 yard Moelwyn tunnel with incidentally, Mathew taking over the now redundant dam and waterwheel to power a slate sawmill to deal with block from his quarry. Obviating the inclines enabled all down working to be by gravity as far as the Cob, where horses which had ridden down in dandy cars, hauled the train the rest of the way, and of course took back the empty wagons to Blaenau. Two or three brakemen rode on the trains of up to 100 trucks or more.

Individual horses did not work the whole distance, intermediate stabling and crossing places allowed them to work the empties back in 4 or 5 stages. Except for the first few months, an outside contractor provided horses and drivers at rates based on tonnage, which initially was 7d

(2.9p) for the entire journey.

This largely gravity operation enforced a different working ethos from the Nantlle. There, when trains of wagons met, it was customary for the one nearest a turn-out to back to it. Dispute as to which was the nearest occasionally being settled by fisticuffs! To avoid the speeding rakes of downgoing F.R. wagons meeting upgoing traffic, disciplined use and adherence to some kind of timetable was called for. This gravity working precluded the collection of tolls on route, so dues were levied by monthly account, an obligation which some quarries were notoriously reluctant to settle. It also differed from the Nantlle in that the F.R. supplied wagons to their customers. When the line opened there was surprisingly little rush to connect to it in spite of the per ton quarry to ship costs being reputedly reduced from 15/- to 5/- (75p to 25p), in fact ten years on, by severely trimming their charges, the hauliers and boatmen still retained almost 50% of their pre-F.R. business. Boating on the Dwyryd survived into the late 1860s when the building of the railway bridge across the estuary made navigation impracticable.

Holland was the sole founder-user of the F.R. but due to a wayleave dispute, he did not have direct incline connection until 1839, a year after Welsh Slate had built theirs. Matthew's Middle Quarry was connected in 1842, followed by the then newly opened Llechwedd (SH700470) in 1848, all of course to the Dinas branch.

Diffwys quarry who were already using a mix of 3' 4½" plateways and 2' 2" edge rails, baulked at the idea of a third gauge, and anyway had their own road. Thus the use of the Duffws branch was mainly confined to Bowydd.

Although not yet a passenger carrier, except for a few private carriages, the significance of the F.R. cannot be overstated. By enabling Blaenau Ffestiniog to become the slate supplier to the world, it made Porthmadog an important commercial, ship building and engineering centre. In fact the latter commenced even before the F.R. opened when Thomas Jones of Caernarfon, having been awarded the contract to supply the chairs for the permanent way, established a foundry in Porthmadog. This foundry, managed by his son John, traded as Glaslyn and survived as a major engineering works up to the 1960s. Neither must it be forgotten that the F.R. supported several lead and other mines as well as non-slate quarrying, both by providing an outlet for product and facilitating engineering back up.

The other significant rail development between 1830 and 1850 occurred in north Caernarfonshire.

When outputs soared following the repeal of the Slate Tax, the Penrhyn Railroad coped well but the Dinorwig Railway did not. Thomas Assheton-Smith II who had inherited Dinorwig in 1828, saw the need to provide a more efficient transport link. He also saw the need to avoid his father's niggardliness which had saddled him with an unsatisfactory rail line. Accordingly a number of engineers and contractors were brought in and given something approaching carte blanche. There was a margin at least part way along the north-eastern shore of Llyn Padarn which might have provided the basis for a lakeside route obviating all question of uphaulage, indeed there are reports of an early tramroad there possibly used by Lord Newborough's Fachwen quarry (SH578615). In fact it was the presence of that quarry which prevented Dinorwig using this obvious route. Hence a line was surveyed, by James Spooner, and some earthworks constructed, which, starting some 300' above the lake would have reduced but not obviated the uphaulage. This route would have swung north to avoid Lord Newborough's land and after some deviation, including tunnelling, would have joined the existing route at about its halfway point. Instead of using the Garth incline, the revised route would have continued on to reach an incline running directly into the harbour area at Port

Dinorwig.

Assheton-Smith cleared the way for a lakeside route by buying Fachwen in 1840 (renaming it Faenol), and by 1843 the **Padarn Railway** was in business. It was of 4' gauge using transporter trucks each carrying four 1' 10¾" gauge quarry wagons to Port Dinorwig with magnificent panache.

Starting alongside Llyn Peris at the foot of the C inclines at Muriau it passed through the Glan y Bala rock by a tunnel to pick up material brought down the A inclines, the two lower pitches of which were turned to meet it at Gilfach Ddu. It ran alongside Llyn Padarn, then across country for almost 7 miles with a constant fall of around 1 in 200 to Penscoins on the scarp behind Port Dinorwig. Here the quarry wagons were off loaded from the transporters and crewled down an incline (partly in a 43 yard long tunnel), to the dockside 300' below.

Initially horse-drawn, it is tempting to suppose that the gauge and gradient profile were chosen to suit the minimum size and maximum capabilities of locomotives of the time. No evidence has been found to support this and a 4' gauge was not unusual for horse tramways, being used for instance in the Whitehaven limeworks at Porthywaen in southern Denbighshire and the Saundersfoot Railway in Pembrokeshire. However when locomotives were introduced in 1848 the layout was so suitable that the only work was the replacement of the stone block sleepers and rail with conventional wooden sleepers carrying chaired rail. In fact apart from a small re-alignment near Faenol and the replacing of the underfloor sheaves and chains with a conventional drum and wire rope at the Penscoins drumhouse, the only major alteration in the whole of its life was moving the terminus to Gilfach Ddu. Material from Muriau then being carried through the tunnel on a horse drawn quarry gauge line, which by 1870 when all engineering was centralised at the Gilfach Ddu workshops, became steam hauled. In 1889 the tunnel was abandoned and the line re-routed around Glan y Bala, sufficient waste having been accumulated to provide a platform to accommodate it.

The steamed Padarn Railway is notable, not only for its early date but for its original Horlock engines, the 0-4-0 frameless Jenny Lind and Fire Queen representing an interesting evolutionary link between the 'Rocket' and the modern locomotive. (Their 1880s/90s replacements were also unusual for quarry lines in being 0-6-0.)

The abandonment of the 1824 line left the Allt Ddu and Chwarel Fawr districts isolated. This was remedied by laying down the Village Tramway to carry their output to the main quarry at what became known as Steam Mills Level, from where it could be sent down the A inclines to Gilfach Ddu. This slightly uphill tramway was replaced by a locomotive line on an altered route at the end of the 19th century.

There was never any public use of the Padarn but workmen were allowed to travel in their own self-built man-powered vehicles. This increased the labour catchment area which eventually included south west Anglesey. Men living there crossed to Port Dinorwig by ferry in the early hours of a Monday, barracking during the week and returning on a Saturday afternoon. Proper workmen's trains were introduced in 1885 from which time the line was usually known as the **Dinorwig Quarries Railway**.

The several writing slate factories at Deiniolen having been nurtured by the original line, continued and even flourished after it closed, surviving until the 1890s. The Efail Castell stable became a general smithy until post WW2. On the new line, the Crawia slate works at Pont Rhythallt (SH536643) developed into an important slate finishing complex.

Slate activity was not quite totally confined to the north of Wales, there being a comparatively small, but long established industry in north Pembrokeshire. The units generally were too small to justify the laying of rails.

In 1841 the Abereiddi (SM795315) and the Porthgain (SM813325) quarries came together under one ownership. Whereas both the shipping and the slate sawing facilities at Porthgain had potential for development, those at Abereiddi did not. Accordingly the 2 mile, 2' (?) gauge, horse drawn **Abereiddi Tramroad** was built in 1851 to convey slates and block from Abereiddi to Porthgain. Since road access to Abereiddi was difficult and Porthgain lacked stacking space, a depot for land sales was established part-way along the line. Disused for part of the 1860s, it was re-built c. 1870, finally becoming derelict in the late 1880s. Of little significance, indeed it has been classed as an internal tramway, but it was the sole narrow gauge slate line in north Pembrokeshire.

4 The 1850s. The Coming of the Standard Gauge

PLUS The Gorseddau, Corris and other Tramways

The first part of the national railway network to enter Wales was the **Chester and Holyhead Railway** (later London & North Western). Having bridged the Conwy, negotiated the dreaded cliffs at Penmaenmawr via two tunnels, it reached Bangor in 1848. There, having bored three more tunnels and built two viaducts, it paused for breath as it were, while Robert Stephenson was spectacularly bridging the Menai Straits.

Being built specifically to improve communications with Ireland, it had little intentional Welsh relevance and apparently no slate significance except as a reminder that it was the railways which were generating the building boom which was fuelling the demand for slate. Since, not only did the railways stimulate the construction of factories, houses and public buildings, but the railways themselves needed stations, warehouses and structures of every kind, all of which had to be roofed, and in many cases slab floored.

With the growth of coaching and of the slate trade, Bangor had quadrupled from a cathedral village to a shipbuilding and slate port. The railway killed the coaching trade, but stimulated general commerce. Despite slate shipments at Hirael being already in decline following the opening of Port Penrhyn, rail connection helped the town to flourish as a slate trading and support centre, with at least four slate finishing works.

The C. & H.R.'s slate impact may have been nil when it opened, but this dramatically changed when Penrhyn quarry built their **Port Penrhyn Branch** from it in 1852. This 1½ mile private line ran from a junction at Llandygái and dropped down to cross the Cegin twice by iron bridges, to run to the port alongside the Penrhyn Railroad. Exchange sidings at the port enabled, for the first time, the delivery of slate to inland destinations without recourse to carts and canals.

Whilst the C. & H.R. had been making its way along the coast, it had been widely predicted that it would fail to cross the Menai and would be forced to abandon Holyhead and divert to Porth Dinllaen. Accordingly the Bangor & Porth Dinllaen Railway was formed to build a line through Caernarfon and tunnel under the Rivals, to establish a route which the C. & H.R. would be forced to use.

The prospect of the Menai bridge becoming a reality, made Porth Dinllaen a dead duck, so the B. & P.D. line renamed the **Bangor and Caernarfon Railway**, was terminated at Caernarfon which it reached in 1852. The 7½ mile line had one tunnel the 497 yard Vaynol, built more because Thomas Assheton-Smith did not wish to have the sight and sound of smelly locomotives interfering with the tranquillity of his Vaynol Park residence, rather than engineering necessity. A somewhat 'nimbyish' attitude for a man who had himself brought the first steam locomotives to north Wales.

The B. & C.R. had stations at Treborth, Griffiths Crossing and, more significantly, Port Dinorwig, where the 1 mile **Port Dinorwig Branch** (actually classed as a siding) was laid in emulation of the Port Penrhyn link.

Whilst the B. & C.R. had some potential to be of value to the small quarries of Cwm Gwyrfai and Llanberis, but being a truncation of the original B. & P.D.R. plan which would have imperiously viaducted the mouth of the Seiont, it was the wrong side of the town to reach the Caernarfon Quays and tap the riches of Nantlle. Thus although it had the important Port Dinorwig connection, its slate significance at Caernarfon was, at least for the time being, slight.

However, the railway was of great social, economic and

political importance to Caernarfon, the first non-industrial Welsh town to have a railway deliberately laid to it. Although the railway failed to further the town's pretensions as a seaside resort (these were of course usurped by the new towns further east), its industrial and commercial impact was considerable. Rail connection helped J.P. de Winton develop the Union Foundry into an engineering and locomotive works of international repute and to encourage the rise of at least half a dozen slate finishers. Such activities led to Caernarfon's considerable enhancement as a trading centre and growth from a local port and county town, into a regional capital.

Despite the B. & C.R.'s lack of success in securing slate business at Caernarfon, the Port Dinorwig and Port Penrhyn branches meant that almost half the total Welsh slate output, had the option of rail distribution. This traffic eventually became so heavy that a depot at Saltney, near Chester, had to be established to handle it.

Fortunately for the indigenous shipping industry, high rail charges meant that much slate continued to go out by coasting vessels. This together with a mounting overseas demand meant that the tonnage shipped at both Port Penrhyn and Port Dinorwig increased so much even after rail connection, that both had to be enlarged and it would be over 30 years before rail tonnages exceeded shipments.

The two short port lines had other impacts, promoting the growth of both ports as industrial sites in their own right. This infrastructure and the fact that coal could be brought in by rail, ending the laborious unloading of it from ships with buckets, helped both Penrhyn and Dinorwig to pioneer the use of steamships for the slate trade. Arising out of this Port Dinorwig would also develop a substantial steamship and locomotive repair business.

Thus paradoxically, this originally totally non-slate Chester & Holyhead Railway was possibly the most influential slate line of all. Not only did it directly further the dominance of Penrhyn and Dinorwig quarries, but in enabling the development of supply, manufacturing and engineering industries, it created something of a 'carpet of prosperity' from Bangor to Caernarfon.

During 1854 and 1855, business confidence was affected by the Crimean war, checking the slate industry's twenty years of gradual growth, but after the treaty of Paris in 1856, the economy bounced back and home and overseas demand combined to put slate working into a period of unbridled expansion.

By this time Blaenau Ffestiniog had overtaken Dyffryn Nantlle as the third largest slate producer after Penrhyn and Dinorwig, and outside of these 'Big Four' areas other quarries were taking advantage of the boom. Besides which, in spite of virtually all the worthwhile locations already being exploited, entrepreneurs spurred by tales of the vast profits being made at Penrhyn were looking for new places to dig. It seems to have been widely believed that if one hacked a hole almost anywhere and threw enough money into it, untold wealth would result.

Such illusions were held by one Von Uster and his north of England backers when they came to Gorseddau (SH573453). This name implies a place where bards impart wisdom, had bards or indeed anyone else, imparted wisdom to these gentlemen, they would not have considered quarrying at this remote and cheerless location, let alone building a grandiose mill, streets of houses and, by 1857, the horse drawn, 3' gauge, 8 mile **Gorseddau Tramway** to Porthmadog.

Within the quarry both 2' and 3' tracks were used, the 2' for rubbish and the carrying of blocks to the slate making sheds, while finished slates together with blocks for the mill went down the exit incline in 3' gauge wagons. From the foot of the incline the line ran from the quarry for about 2½ miles to an unique multi-storey mill. Here a triangular junction enabled finished slates made at the quarry to pass on down the line, while block ran into the mill for conversion to slab products, which could then join the roofing slates for the circuitous journey to Porthmadog.

At Tremadog it joined, via a reversing switchback, the disused Portmadoc & Penmorfa Railway. This late 1830s 1½ mile 3' gauge tramway ran to the Llidart Ysbyty ironstone mine (SH556402). The gauge of this tramway, and hence the Gorseddau, may have been determined by its having made use of Porthmadog Cob tramway trackwork which had become redundant when the Ffestiniog Railway was laid across the Cob. The Gorseddau continued to Porthmadog making use of the trackbed of the old line which ran alongside the Tremadog canal. This waterway was originally a drain which was allegedly accorded canal status by Madocks to lend prestige to Tremadog. It did in fact actually accommodate sea-going vessels, which probably brought in coal and possibly took out product from the Tremadog woollen mill.

At Porthmadog the Gorseddau diverged from the Tremadog route, taking a more direct course to join the Ffestiniog Railway tracks at the harbour.

Although one of the best engineered of all slate tramways, it was the least trafficked. Like the Penrhyn and Dinorwig lines it was one quarry's private line, but it did also serve one or two tiny independent quarries and possibly a peat turbary, as well as carrying supplies as return loads. There was one passenger carriage for the quarry's private use, but no public passenger service. But with over thirty families living in the quarry village of Treforus, plus men barracking, plus an indigenous population, there must have been some unofficial carriage of people. In addition one can imagine travelling salesmen who were such a prominent feature of rural Caernarfonshire at the time, riding in trucks perched self-importantly on their sample-cases.

However, the quarry's era was brief and unsuccessful, even at its 1860 peak, it would have been a good week if much more than a dozen wagons went down to Porthmadog and well before the end of the decade it would have been a good week if even one wagon arrived there.

In the south of Gwynedd, as yet without main line railways, four tramways were laid down to shipping points in the late 1850s. The **Arthog** quarry (SH650151) line was a mere ½ mile, almost all incline. The **Fron Goch** quarry (SH664972) had an even shorter hand pushed line. A third, the **Tyddyn Sieffre** tramway was more substantial running from the quarry at SH630135 via a self-acting incline and a mile long horse-drawn run across the flood plain to a wharf at SH634149. Of these, Fron Goch boated to Aberdyfi, the other two to Barmouth. All were 2' gauge.

The fourth line was an altogether different affair. For centuries slate from Corris, Aberllefenni and the Dulas valley had been shipped at Derwen-las (SN722991), a tiny port on the southern bank of the river Dyfi which served Machynlleth and much of western Montgomeryshire. From the mid 1830s road improvements had spurred the growth of slate working at Corris itself, but the long and expensive cartage limited the competitiveness of its products. In addition, R.D. Pryce the energetic proprietor of the Aberllefenni quarry (SH768103) had by mid-century, almost monopolised the limited wharfage at Derwen-las which, in any case, could only handle vessels of up to about 70 tons.

Therefore the first rail proposal, the Aberdovey Railway of 1850 ignored the south side of the river altogether. It was to commence at Aberllefenni quarry's old mill (the present 'Village' mill did not then exist), run down the west side of the Llefenni valley to Aberllefenni village and along the north side of the road to Corris. Then after being joined by a siding from 'Magnus works', the enamelling factory at SH768091, it would have crossed to the south of the road to pass through Corris village. A branch from Ty'n y Berth quarry (SH738087) at Upper Corris would join it a quarter mile beyond.

It was to run close, and to the north west of the Machynlleth road with a short tunnel through the bluff at SH752044. Passing behind the houses at the end of the Dyfi bridge, it would cross to the south of the Aberdyfi road and follow low-lying ground to Ynys (SN688983) where there was to be a branch to the river. Despite its name the proposal did not extend to Aberdyfi, terminating at SN664971, at what would presumably have been an enlargement of the Fron Goch quarry jetty.

This idea was recycled in 1852 as the Corris, Machynlleth & Aberdovey Railway, substantially unaltered except that it was to have an extra branch to Tycan at the head of the Ceiswyn valley to serve the Ratgoed quarry at SH787119. The potential traffic from Hafodty (SH725064) and Drainllwydion (SH721058) slate quarries was cited as additional justification for running to the north of the Dyfi. Presumably in recognition of the shortcomings of Fron Goch as a shipping point, a futher revision was put forward as the Corris, Machynlleth, Aberdyfi & Towyn Railway. Its route was the same, except that the Ynys branch was deleted, and via two short tunnels would have pressed on to Aberdyfi (where there was to be a dock branch) and on to Tywyn following approximately the route followed by the subsequent main line railway.

This main line, the Aberystwyth and Welch Coast Railway, was still a decade away. So was its connecting Newtown & Machynlleth Railway, but at this time it was the Shrewsbury & Aberystwyth Railway which was bidding to run to Machynlleth. Anticipating its arrival, the C.M.A. & T.R. proposal included a branch to it, crossing the river just downstream of Dyfi bridge. A further refinement considered by the C.M.A. & T.R., was an extension from Upper Corris to Tir Stint iron mine at SH760164.

In the end the whole north bank idea was abandoned and the 1859, 8 mile, horse drawn **Corris, Machynlleth and River Dovey Tramroad** adhered to tradition and ran to Derwen-las, the accommodation problems there being avoided by pushing on a further half mile to Quay Ward which was already in use by several lead mining companies and where in 1845 Arthur Coulston owner of Braich Goch quarry (SH748078) and a prime backer of the line, had already established a slate wharf. Following the opening of the Corris line other wharves were rented by the Talyllyn United Slate Company then briefly operating Gaewern quarry (SH745086) and the Ty'n y Berth Slate Quarry Company. Quay Ward also served Morben quarry (SN716993) whose capacious powder house acted as a communal magazine for all the tramroad users.

There was a proposal for an extension to Garreg about a mile down river from Quay Ward, where boats of up to 700 tons could lie, or even on to a new wharf at Glandyfi which could handle even larger vessels and be less tide-dependent. It could also have served Glandyfi quarry (SN698961), but the whole scheme was overtaken by the anticipated arrival of the Aberystwyth & Welch Coast Railway.

The C.M. & R.D. route down the Dulas valley, was of course built mainly as a roadside line on the south east of the Corris-Machynlleth road. A plan for a line up the west side of the Llefenni valley was scrapped, the line being terminated at Aberllefenni village at SH770098, close to the quarry's new mill. The quarry itself was reached by a short branch on the east of the valley, an 1870s proposal to extend this branch to Cambergi quarry (SH765108) falling through when that quarry failed. The 2 mile **Ratgoed Tramway** which ran from the eponymous quarry to join end-on at Aberllefenni and the Ty'n y Berth tramway (afterwards the **Upper Corris Tramway**) were both built as originally envisaged in the 1852 C.M. & A.R. proposal. Interestingly the Ratgoed was the sole means of communication for the quarry settlement, neighbouring farms and the shop which catered for just half a dozen households. Passenger carrying on this branch (on hand-pushed flat trucks!), antedated passenger carrying on tramroad proper.

None of the actual Corris quarries were directly served by the C.M. & R.D. main line, all being connected via the mile long Upper Corris tramway. It joined the main line at Maespoeth (SH755073). South of this, short branches at Ceinws and Llwyngwern served quarries at SH760064 and SH757045 respectively. The whole layout was in 2' 3" gauge, the reason for this slightly non-standard figure may have been because it was already in use at Aberllefenni quarry.

This line gave the quarries it served transport facilities which were comparable with Blaenau's and converted the Corris hamlet into a 'Mini Blaenau Ffestiniog'. Unfortunately although the slate market was then booming and Corris' product especially its slab, was second to none, the tardiness of the area's entry into the market, meant that its quarries had some difficulty in finding acceptance as prime suppliers.

Over in north-east Wales a number of quarries had, since early in the century, been able to use the Montgomeryshire and Llangollen canals but it was 1856 before any could reach them by rail.

That year the **Oernant Tramway** opened to serve the quarries near the Horseshoe Pass north of Llangollen. This 3 mile line ran from Moel y Faen quarry (SJ185477) to a short incline at Clogau quarry (SJ185463). From there it dropped by a second, much longer incline, to run down the mile or so to the Llangollen canal at Pentrefelin (SJ218436), where water from the river Dee powered a mill for sawing slate block. (No water for power was available at the Horseshoe Pass quarries) Although by this time 2' or thereabouts was becoming universal, the line was laid to 3' to conform to existing quarry tracks.

The Oernant never officially carried general freight but reputedly supplies in upgoing empty wagons greatly eased life for the quarry families living in the bleak and remote quarry cottages at Moel y Faen and in the nearby settlement at Maesyrychen.

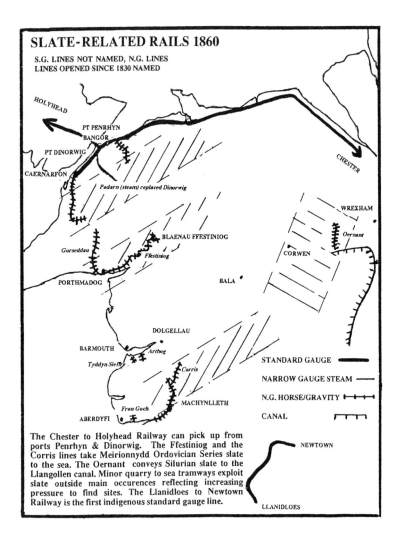

SLATE-RELATED RAILS 1860

S.G. LINES NOT NAMED, N.G. LINES
LINES OPENED SINCE 1830 NAMED

HOLYHEAD

PT PENRHYN
BANGOR
PT DINORWIG
CAERNARFON

CHESTER

Padarn (steam) replaced Dinorwig

WREXHAM

Oernant

BLAENAU FFESTINIOG

CORWEN

Gorseddau

Ffestiniog

PORTHMADOG

BALA

DOLGELLAU

BARMOUTH

Arthog

Tyddyn Sieffre

Corris

MACHYNLLETH

Fron Goch

ABERDYFI

STANDARD GAUGE	▬▬▬
NARROW GAUGE STEAM	———
N.G. HORSE/GRAVITY	┣━┿━┥
CANAL	┌┬┬┐

The Chester to Holyhead Railway can pick up from
ports Penrhyn & Dinorwig. The Ffestiniog and the
Corris lines take Meirionnydd Ordovician Series slate
to the sea. The Oernant conveys Silurian slate to the
Llangollen canal. Minor quarry to sea tramways exploit
slate outside main occurences reflecting increasing
pressure to find sites. The Llanidloes to Newtown
Railway is the first indigenous standard gauge line.

NEWTOWN

LLANIDLOES

5 The 1860s. Blaenau Ffestiniog

By the 1860s the Blaenau Ffestiniog slate quarries had become a force to be reckoned with. Ever since quarry proprietor Nathaniel Mathew had famously obtained orders for the re-roofing of Hamburg after the 1842 fire, its influence particularly in overseas markets had explosively grown. By the late 1850s slate traffic to Porthmadog exceeded 50,000 tons per annum, almost double the tonnage at the time the F.R. opened in 1836. With buyers increasingly specifying 'Portmadoc' slate rather than 'Bangor', the dominance of Penrhyn and Dinorwig was being challenged and well before the end of the 1860s Blaenau's tonnages would exceed 100,000, outstripping these two erstwhile market leaders.

Diffwys quarry had in 1860, at last bowed to the inevitable and like its neighbouring Maenofferen (SH715467), Bowydd (SH708462) and Foty (SH707468) quarries, was sending output down inclines to join the Ffestiniog Railway at Duffws. Two years later Wrysgan (SH678456) was directly connected to the F.R. by an epic incline dropping 800' partly in tunnel to Tanygrisiau. Less significant, but even more visually spectacular, was the Moelwyn incline of the revived Moelwyn quarry (SH661442), under a mile long it dropped over 1000' by a dramatic cascade of 7 inclines.

Although there were annoying hold-ups, particularly the non-return of empty wagons, the F.R. coped surprisingly well with this increased traffic. However the F.R. directors' collective nightmare was that one day someone would build a steam railway to Blaenau which would offer a better service and lower rates. For the F.R. to use steam on a 2' gauge line did not seem to be an option neither was re-gauging the existing route. Contingency plans included building a new line northwards to a dock at Deganwy on the Conwy estuary which could also join the L. & N.W.R. at

Llandudno Junction, foreshadowing the 1870s L. & N.W.R. route to Blaenau.

From 1850, there had been piecemeal improvements. Track having been upgraded from the original fishbelly rails, a sharp bend at Tanygrisiau was eased by building an embankment across a corner of the lake, and another at Garnedd rock just above the present Tan y Bwlch station was straightened by cutting a 60 yard tunnel. To further assist gravity running there were also ideas of easing the curve at Hafod y Llyn by boring a 138 yard tunnel, but this seemed to go beyond what they could be expected to do merely to benefit their captive customers, whom they regarded as a pretty stroppy lot anyway.

In the early 1860s, that most forceful of railway builders, Thomas Savin announced that immediately his **Aberystwyth & Welch Coast Railway** reached Porthmadog he would lay a branch to Blaenau. This branch would have left the main line just west of Penrhyndeudraeth, climbed up to Rhyd crossed to the south west of the F.R., and terminated in the southern part of Blaenau itself. How serious was Savin's intention is unknown but it stung the F.R. into an immediate decision to steam the line and to hastily invite quotations for locomotives. Although a number of firms tendered, the loco contract was awarded to George England who was a friend of Charles Holland, nephew of Samuel Holland. Charles Holland has been credited with the design of the initial batch of four, but England had to tone down Holland's ideas, such as substituting 0-4-0 for Hollands' 0-6-0. These first locos, (The) Prince, (The) Princess, Mountaineer and Palmerston proved disappointing when they entered service in 1863/64, and they were eventually, much modified, confined to shunting duties. Despite this, their general arrangement became a prototype for narrow gauge locomotives everywhere.

The 1863 conversion of the F.R. to steam followed by the successful introduction of the 0-4-4-0 Double Fairlie locomotives, Little Wonder (1869) and James Spooner (1872), marked north west Wales' move from a technically imitative culture to a technically innovative culture. This change, was emphasised by the F.R.'s pioneering bogie carriages and wagons of 1872 and 1874, and totally vindicated when the Double Fairlies, Myrddin Emrys and Livingstone Thompson were built in-house in 1879 and 1885 respectively. It was purely due to economics, and not to any shortcomings of Boston Lodge works, that, until they built the Earl of Merioneth in 1979, all subsequent engines were bought in.

In 1865 a passenger service was begun, the first ever on any sub-standard gauge steam railway, carrying in its first full year of operation a quarter of a million people. At Blaenau there were passenger stations on both branches, served by alternate trains, but since Dinas station only served a handful of dwellings inexorably being engulfed by advancing quarry spoil, it was closed in 1870 leaving Duffws as the sole passenger terminus.

Apart from ending the social and economic isolation of Blaenau Ffestiniog, the passenger capabilities of the steamed F.R. proved vital to the quarries' manning needs. Every additional 1000 tons of annual output called for at least 25 extra men which with families, added up to 100 or more persons. Already desperately overcrowded, no way could the town have housed the extra numbers which the explosively expanding quarries demanded, let alone the shopkeepers, tradesmen, publicans and parsons needed to serve and support them. The railway enabled men living as far away as Porthmadog to travel to work daily and appreciably widened the catchment for weekly barrackers and lodgers. Not only did it bring Porthmadog to within about an hour's travel of Blaenau, but also when in 1867 the A. & W.C. reached Porthmadog, 'Breakfast in Blaenau – Tea in London' became a reality, a far cry from the times, barely outside living memory, of Blaenau quarry owners walking to London to sell slates.

As the town continued to expand, the steamed F.R. proved vital in bringing in food and general supplies to support the burgeoning population. The town's bakeries were supplied with flour milled at Porthmadog from grain brought in by sea. The line also carried coal both for the town and for the dozens of fuel-hungry quarry boilers.

All this time there were Blaenau quarries which being high up to the east of Mynydd Manod, had lacked rail connection. The 1854 F.R. backed Festiniog & Machno Railway, from Duffws to Cwm Machno quarry (SH751470) would have catered for all of them, but it was not pursued. The steaming of the F.R. was an incentive to rectify this lack, the **Rhiwbach Tramway** opening in 1863.

This 3½ mile line did not reach Cwm Machno, but terminated at Rhiwbach quarry (SH740462), whose then owners, the Festiniog Slate Company footed the bill for its construction. Besides Rhiwbach the line served three other quarries which had been laboriously and expensively boating from Maentwrog.

At Rhiwbach itself an incline powered by the mill engine raised outgoing trucks almost 200' to the start of the tramway. This mill engine also uphauled the underground incline, wound a short surface incline and, briefly, a vertical shaft as well.

After making its way at well over 1600' above sea level for a few hundred yards, the main tramway was joined by a branch descending, via a reversing switchback, from Bwlch y Slaters quarry (SH732455) 80' above the line. It then passed Blaen y Cwm quarry (SH735463), which reached it via an uphaulage incline driven from the engine which provided back-up power to the water-driven mill.

After ½ mile the line was joined by the short spur from Cwt y Bugail quarry (SH734469). No incline was required, but the slight up gradient was rope-worked, again from the mill engine. The earlier scheme would have continued on past Cwt y Bugail, reaching Cwm Machno quarry (SH751470) by a water balance. Although expensive, this would have been of immense value to Cwm Machno and other quarries in the Machno valley, but the endemic lack of water at this height would have made it a non-starter. In spite of several proposals for railways up the Machno valley, the quarries there were never rail connected.

The Rhiwbach line ran with a slight down gradient, maintained by cuttings, tunnels and a bridge over the Bowydd, to the head of an incline high above Blaenau Ffestiniog. This incline dropped down some 250' to Maenofferen quarry and after a short level section a further incline, which also carried Maenofferen output, dropped down another 300'.

From here the tramway took over a pre-existing route from Bowydd quarry and ran along the contour before dropping down almost 300' to make a junction with the F.R. at Duffws station.

Although never officially a passenger or general goods carrier this branch did serve a support function for the settlement around Rhiwbach quarry. It brought supplies to the village shop (latterly from Brymers, a large store in Blaenau). Additionally purchases made by housewives in Blaenau on Saturdays were brought up on the Monday's first rake of empties, as was at one time the Blaenau-based mistress of the tiny Rhiwbach school. When in the 1920s petrol driven locos replaced horses on the summit section there was some semi-official carriage of workmen. In latter years both the between-incline levels were worked by I.C. locos.

The need to provide railed transport for slate originating in the Llan Ffestiniog area by a link to the F.R. had been recognised for some time. The steaming of the F.R. now made such a line an attractive proposition.

In 1868 on the initiative of Samuel Holland and other

quarry owners, the **Festiniog and Blaenau Railway** was opened. This 2' gauge 3½ mile steam line although acting as a feeder to the Ffestiniog Railway was entirely independent of it and their relationships with it were never of the best. Also their two 0-4-2 Manning Wardle locos owed little to F.R. thinking.

Starting from a terminus at Llan Ffestiniog, it endeavoured to chase the contours to the village of Manod and thence to Dolgarregddu station in Blaenau itself. An onward connection linked with the adjacent Duffws arm of the F.R. also served the Newborough writing slate factory on the Bowydd at SH699457. The F. & B.R. also served a writing slate factory at SH706453 near Manod Station.

For such a short and apparently easy route the civil work was substantial, calling for cuttings, embankments and numerous bridges, including at Manod, a four span 320' wooden viaduct. Even so grades in places were a stiff 1 in 68.

Slate traffic from Llan was never great, the few quarries in its vicinity were small and the nearest being almost 2 miles from the station made feeder line connection out of the question. Two quarries Foel Gron (SH744428) & Bryn Glas (SH732423) eventually built tramways to their respective adjacent roads and Nantypistyll Gwyn quarry (SH751433) started but never completed a similar link.

The F. & B.'s main slate traffic came from Graig Ddu quarry (SH724454) which immediately made enthusiastic use of it, replacing the steep road via which their carters had eventually reached the Dwyryd, by a four-pitch incline joining the F. & B. at its Manod station. This cascade which if one adds the short incline within the quarry, descended 1400' was surely the finest in the industry, and thanks to the 'Ceir Gwyllt', was unique in being 'passenger carrying'.

These 'Wild Cars' consisted of a 'skateboard' which ran on the left-hand rail of the right-hand track, steadied by an arm carrying a tiny wheel which bore on the right-hand rail of the left-hand track. There was a rudimentary brake but speeds were high, accidents frequent and fatalities not unknown. Users would carry small children as a treat (?) and occasionally two or even three adults, would share one car. It is said that the Rhiwbach schoolmistress referred to above, returned home at the end of the day by this route!

The F. & B. also picked up granite from Pengwern quarry (SH706447) by a spur off the Graig Ddu feeder but its overwhelming significance lay in its offering a full passenger and goods service to Llan Ffestiniog, thus halting the marginalisation of this traditionally important township and putting it in touch with Blaenau, and via the F.R. with Porthmadog, by now very much a Regional Capital. It also provided a further widening of Blaenau's labour catchment area.

Close to Blaenau Ffestiniog, but topographically isolated from it in a remote hanging valley, the inhabitants of the tiny village of Croesor scratched a living from agriculture and some occasional slate working. Its prosperity seemed assured when the ancient road passing through it was turnpiked in 1801, but when this Maentwrog to Beddgelert route was supplanted by a turnpike via Rhyd and Llanfrothen in 1812, the road north of Croesor fell into disuse leaving the hamlet at a dead end (the present road up to Croesor from Garreg is a much later construction).

In the 1850s, near the col between Cwm Croesor and Cwm Orthin, Rhosydd quarry (SH664461) was being developed. This quarry had originally sent output by pack animal along a precipitous track which skirted Moelwyn Mawr to join up with the Moelwyn quarry's track down to the Maentwrog-Beddgelert road at Rhyd. By making improvements in the track down Cwm Orthin they could theoretically cart to the Ffestiniog Railway at Tanygrisiau, but this was dependent on Cwm Orthin quarry (SH681459) allowing wheeled vehicles to cross their land, a courtesy they rarely extended.

In 1856 there had been an imaginative scheme to drive an 800 yard tramway tunnel eastwards from Rhosydd's 5 Level (i.e. about halfway vertically between the top of the quarry and the eventual main tunnel on level 9). It would emerge above Cwm Orthin which it would have reached by two inclines, descending to the F.R. at Tanygrisiau by a further two. In order to obtain compulsory powers to slightly encroach onto Cwm Orthin quarry territory it was to be constructed under a Railway Act. Had this gone through there would have been the curious anomaly of a mile of private narrow gauge mineral line, almost entirely either tunnel or incline, being legally the equal of say the Great Western Railway.

The need for such an expensive scheme seemed obviated in 1860 when the Cwm Orthin quarry closed, enabling plans to be hastily drawn for a railway along the route of the Cwm Orthin cart track. This idea was scotched within weeks when Cwm Orthin re-opened and within a year had built their **Cwmorthin Tramway** down to Tanygrisiau. This 1 mile line which had two inclines plus a third within the quarry area, was strictly no-go territory for any competitor. Thus Rhosydd had to continue to reach its siding at Tanygrisiau by packhorse.

By the early 1860s alongside Rhosydd a second quarry, Croesor (SH657457), was being developed, and in 1864 Hugh Beaver Roberts, its landlord and part backer, opened the 2' gauge, 8 mile **Croesor Tramway** from the head of Cwm Croesor to Porthmadog. Croesor quarry which until then had had a daunting cross-country struggle to reach the F.R. was connected to the new tramway by a precipitous incline with Rhosydd doing likewise. These inclines each with a fall of about 750' were the two highest single-pitch inclines in Wales.

At a ¼ mile from the foot of the inclines, the tramway dropped the 150' to the valley floor via the Blaen y Cwm incline. From there it ran along the valley floor for 1½ miles to Croesor village, the only engineering being three exceptionally fine clapper bridges.

Part way along, the line was joined in 1879 by the two pitch Pant Mawr incline which served the quarry of that name at SH658446. Circa 1890 Pant Mawr's workings having been developed downwards to become Fron Boeth quarry, the upper pitch of the incline was abandoned and the lower extended to meet a contour chasing line which connected to the Fron Boeth workings by way of a unique tunnel. At or near Croesor village, several small quarries were able to load onto the tramway, Parc Slab quarry (SH632444) being subsequently connected by a short branch.

From Croesor village the grade was maintained for ½ mile, partially on a fine stone embankment to the head of the two pitch Parc incline. This incline dropped the line almost 500' to the Glaslyn flood plain. Here, from 1872 a branch joined from Parc quarry (SH626436) via two short inclines on the south side of Afon Croesor.

Other than the crossing of the Afon Glaslyn, there was then a flat, uneventful 4 mile run to join F.R. metals at Porthmadog quays. Part of this final stretch was on Creasy's 1800 embankment which preceded the Cob. Planned but not built was an extension from Porthmadog to Borth-y-gest and a branch to Beddgelert. It was also planned to use locomotives between Porthmadog and the foot of the Parc inclines. Ownership of this flood-plain section passed to a succession of companies with Roberts retaining just the inclines and Croesor valley track.

The Croesor remained a modest line, unambitiously serving its quarry customers. It owned no wagons, users being required to supply their own. Horses and drivers were hired, users being charged for their services on a ton/mile basis. Although fireplaces in the drum-houses indicate an intention to employ permanent brakesmen, the inclines were operated by the horse drivers.

Other than on the Garreg Hylldrem-Porthmadog section after its incorporation into the Welsh highland Railway in the 1920s, the Croesor never carried passengers, but as a general carrier it was of much greater importance than its limited scope would suggest. It provided a vital goods service to Croesor village, and enabled farm materials to be moved along the roadless Croesor valley, a function the line unofficially continued to fulfil long after it fell into disuse in the 1930s.

In addition, sidings on the lower section handled goods for adjoining settlements. The Ynysfor siding at SH605423 served Llanfrothen and the Garreg Hylldrem siding at SH615431 served Nanmor and slate quarries such as Gerynt (SH631484). The Pont Portreuddyn (later Pont Croesor) siding at SH592413 catered for Prenteg, Beddgelert and Nant Gwynant including Hafod y Llan quarry (SH613524), as well as, ephemerally, the Moel Hebog copper mine (SH559472).

An unusual and highly unofficial further use is spoken of. It is said that women from Llanfrothen would 'borrow' trucks from Ynysfor siding to use as 'shopping trolleys' to carry children and groceries home from Porthmadog!

6 The 1860s. The Coast at all costs!

The 1860s was the great decade of railway building in Wales. The nearly 700 standard gauge route miles opened between 1860 and 1869, much more than doubled the existing mileage and was almost twice as much as was ever subsequently laid.

It was the decade when proliferating country stations with their goods and produce handling facilities, livestock pens and in some cases lineside marts, impacted on rural prosperity.

It was also the decade when travelling by train became if not altogether commonplace, at least unremarkable. Even 'Parliamentary' travellers, now renamed third class, were finding their custom encouraged by the offering of some measure of creature comforts.

However, above all it was the decade of the local railway sponsors, gentry such as Sir Watkin Williams-Wynne and G.H. Whalley, engineers such as Benjamin Piercy, but overwhelmingly it was the decade of the contractor-cum-entrepreneurs, Davies and Savin, whose rails arrogantly challenged the might of the G.W.R. and the L. & N.W.R.

While still little more than a jack-of-all-trades in the small village of Llandinam, David Davies had cheekily bid to build part of the Newtown & Llanidloes Railway. By the time it opened in 1859 he had built almost all of it. By 1863, his **Newtown & Machynlleth Railway** had reached across the middle of Wales. He disdainfully sliced a 120' deep chasm through the rock at Talerddig which had hitherto discouraged any thought of a railway following this route by which the Montgomeryshire hinterland traditionally reached the sea. The potential slate significance of this railway was clearly recognised by R.D. Pryce of Aberllefenni quarry, who subscribed heavily and became a director.

In 1864 this line, came together with lines to Oswestry and Wrexham to become the nucleus of the Cambrian

Railways, by which time Davies's associate, Thomas Savin, a flamboyant Oswestry draper turned colliery owner, had struck out on his own to press on with the **Aberystwyth & Welch Coast Railway** which was to establish a chain of rails and hotels around Cardigan Bay from Aberystwyth to Pwllheli and on to Porth Dinllaen. Although aiming to develop the tourist potential of the A. & W.C.R., Savin was also aware that Port Penrhyn and Port Dinorwig were providing the L. & N.W.R. with increasing tonnages of slates and that there were opportunities to do the same thing at Porthmadog.

The line was built in three stages, the first from an end-on junction with the Newtown-Machynlleth line at Machynlleth, along the south bank of the Dyfi towards Aberystwyth. At the same time he started another from the comparatively important port of Aberdyfi to Tywyn and on north to Fairbourne on the south of the Mawddach estuary. The third section progressed north from Barmouth.

In the meantime high in the hills in the hinterland of Tywyn, near the head of the Gwernol valley, Bryneglwys and Cantrebedd farms were the source of good but relatively inaccessible slate. It was possible to sledge their outputs down to Abergynolwyn and thence down the Dysynni valley to Tywyn, but since Tywyn's Gwalia creek could only handle vessels of about a dozen tons, the usual route was by packhorse across the mountain to the Dyfi at Llyn Bwtri (SN703996), which could be used by vessels of perhaps 50 tons.

In 1864 these quarries were taken by a group of north of England men seeking diversification from a cotton trade suffering from the American Civil War. They amalgamated the workings as the Bryneglwys quarry (SH695054) and set about building a railway.

There had previously been ideas for a railway from these quarries to Aberdyfi via Tywyn, which beside conveying slate, would end the relative isolation of Tywyn. This later notion had been overtaken by events in 1863 when the Aberystwyth and Welch Coast Railway joined the two towns.

Thus the **Talyllyn Railway** which opened in 1866 was terminated at exchange sidings on the A. & W.C. at Tywyn, so becoming the first slate quarry railroad to run to a railhead and not to a port.

Its gauge of 2' 3" was apparently chosen to match the neighbouring Corris line, with which there were vague ideas of making connection. It is noteworthy that when the Corris opened in 1859, steam traction was not a serious option. In 1864 when the Talyllyn line was planned the Ffestiniog's technology had, in a few months, gained such a strong prototypal influence that locomotive power was an automatic choice. Their two first Fletcher Jennings engines, Talyllyn and Dolgoch (originally both 0-4-0), are still in service.

At 6½ miles the route was shorter than the F.R., and its topography did not call for the F.R.'s tunnels and tight radii. Only the crossing of the Dolgoch valley required serious bridging, its viaduct being a notable example of railway engineering.

Gradients were modest since although the quarry is at 1000' amsl, most of the fall was accommodated within the Gwernol valley by the Boundary, Beudynewydd, Cantrybedd and Alltwyllt inclines, arriving at the start of the railway proper at Abergynolwyn only 200' above Tywyn Wharf station.

Although built by quarry proprietors for their own convenience, it was a public line serving an obvious and valuable social function along a hitherto isolated valley. A branch running down an incline to Abergynolwyn village brought supplies to the shop and beer to the pub. Uniquely it also ran to each quarry-owned dwelling, enabling coal to be delivered, and night soil removed. This branch also enabled a writing slate factory to be sited in the village, which could provide employment for elderly men, sparing them the stiff walk up to the quarry. In many respects the Talyllyn layout replicated the Gorseddau of the 1850s in being part of an imaginative quarry and railway scheme sponsored by entrepreneurs new to the slate industry. Although the Talyllyn was immeasurably more successful than the Gorseddau, its peak of 8000 tons or so per annum was insufficient to repay the railway's constructional costs. With the intermediate stations, Dolgoch, Brynglas (or Pandy) and Rhydronen being at tiny hamlets, passenger potential was limited. Despite this and its Tywyn terminus, Pendre, being on the edge of the town, annual passenger totals soon reached 20,000, a figure which was maintained until the mid-1920s.

After the McConnels, the original developers, had retired hurt in 1911, when slate output was a quarter of its peak, the local landowner, Sir Haydn Jones recognising the social importance of quarry and railway, bought them both, and subsidised them until his death in 1950.

Not far away in the upper Dyfi valley and working the same vein as Bryneglwys, the small but innovative Minllyn quarry (SH852139) was becoming uncompetitive through lack of rail connection. The landowner, Sir Edmund Buckley stepped in, opening the **Mawddwy Railway** in 1867. This 7 mile line ran from Dinas Mawddwy to Cemmaes Road on the Newtown-Machynlleth section, of what was now the Cambrian Railways. Originally it was intended to be of the same 2' 3" gauge as the Talyllyn, but since so little engineering work was required, standard gauge was chosen to avoid transhipment at Cemmaes Road. It was never profitable, but Sir Edmund also recognising the line's importance to the whole community, underwrote its losses. It closed to passengers in 1901 and to freight in 1908. It was taken by the Cambrian and reopened as a light railway in

1910.

Of the intermediate stations, Mallwyd, Aberangell and Cemmaes, only Aberangell was of any consequence, mainly because of the curious feeder line, the **Hendre Ddu Tramway**. This rather ramshackle and informal affair was built in 1867 to carry the output of Hendre Ddu quarry (SH799125) the 3½ miles to Aberangell station. Three or four other quarries afterwards reached it by branches, and one or two farms may have had spurs. More importantly it opened up this roadless valley assisting farming and facilitating forestry, this latter was very active during both WW1 and WW2 and spawned an additional branch. The original route through Aberangell village was relaid in a more direct line in 1897.

The gauge was variously quoted as 1' 11" or as 2'. Up to 1922 when Hendre Ddu quarry, by that time almost the only user, bought a Simplex petrol loco, the line was horse drawn. Petrol locos were used for forestry work during WW1, and a diesel loco during WW2.

There does not seem to have been any regular passenger or goods traffic on this little line, but clearly few though the residents of the valley were, they would need to travel to market and to shop. Workmen were carried in open cars and from around 1880 these were occasionally used for tourist excursions.

The slate products it carried included large slabs such as billiards table beds. As on the Corris line, these were carried on dedicated wagons having a central supporting rail, the load being secured on either side by poles slotted vertically into apertures on each side of the wagons and tensioned together by ropes at their tops.

In the late 1850s while David Davies was just starting his epic railway career, Henry Robertson whose railway building had brought him to the Wrexham area and the ownership of Brymbo Ironworks, also recognised the potential for railways in the more rural areas and on the coast of Wales, particularly where there were opportunities to carry slate. However unlike Davies and his backers and associates, rather than defying the big companies he made use of them, harnessing the Great Western Railway's ambitions to reach Gwynedd by fronting for them with a series of companies to push rails westward by stealthy stages.

These ambitions thwarted by the collapse of the Worcester & Port Dinllaen scheme and their failure to gain control of the Chester & Holyhead Railway, became personal in 1865 when Daniel Gooch (later Sir Daniel, Bart., MP), marked his transition from Locomotive Superintendent, to Chairman of the Great Western, by putting money into slate quarrying on his son Henry's behalf.

Like Davies, Robertson made use of surveys arising out of the Drummond Commission, but whereas Davies had followed the traditional trade route between eastern Montgomeryshire and the Dyfi, Robertson started out along Telford's Holyhead route (now the A5). His Vale of Llangollen Railway ran from the G.W.R. at Rhosymedre south of Ruabon reaching Llangollen in 1862, where half a mile to the west of the town, sidings at Pentrefelin would offer an alternative to the canal for the slate brought down the Oernant tramway. The next stage, the Llangollen & Corwen Railway was completed in 1865, making a junction with, and thus barring any extension of, the L. & N.W.R.'s Vale of Clwyd branch (which had incidentally, been built by Davies and Savin). The L. & C. first assumed slate significance in 1868 when Penarth quarry (SJ107424) put in an incline connection which enabled it to expand to meet the then burgeoning demand, and uphaul coal for its producer gas plant.

The third stage was to have been the Corwen, Bala and Portmadoc Railway, which departing from Telford's road, would have run to Bala, up the Tryweryn valley and across country to Porthmadog. However with the Aberystwyth & Welch Coast Railway homing in on Porthmadog, redirecting to Blaenau Ffestiniog was considered, but in the event it was terminated at Bala. Opening as the Corwen & Bala railway in 1868, it made an end on junction with the just-completed Bala & Dolgellau Railway south of Bala. The B. & D. was not a Robertson line but was similarly G.W.R. backed and like the other three lines, it had no rolling stock or locos, these being supplied and operated by the G.W.R.

Although a branch south to Corris, climbing up through Brithdir, had been planned, the B. & D. had no direct slate interest, but the Corwen & Bala did pick a little slate at Llandderfel station from Cletwr (SN666921) and possibly neighbouring quarries. It is of interest that when Robertson retired, he built the magnificent Pale house at Llandderfel, going on to crown his career by hosting Queen Victoria on one of her very rare ventures into Wales. The house was lit by a pioneering hydro-electric plant, powered by damming the by then abandoned Cletwr quarry.

These four lines collectively formed the **Ruabon-Dolgellau** branch, the B. & D. being fully incorporated into the G.W.R. in 1877 and the Robertson lines in 1896.

Back at the coast, the Aberystwyth and Welch Coast Railway had reached Aberystwyth in 1864, giving a continuous route to Aberystwyth from Newtown and the UK railway network. This was not immediately of great slate significance but later the line would handle slate slab from Glandyfi (SN698961) and other quarries, with Aberystwyth becoming something of a slate slab centre with three substantial factories. It was partly to cater for this business that in 1874 Aberystwyth harbour was upgraded and connected to the Manchester & Milford Railway (which had reached Aberystwyth from Carmarthen in 1867). It was undoubtedly partly slate which motivated the Worcester & Aberystwyth Junction Railway scheme of 1872 as well as the

1897 East & West Wales Railway which sought to extend the Leominster-New Radnor branch there by a ruler-on-map route that seems to have almost ignored physical obstacles!

To join up the three separate sections of his coastal line, Savin went ahead with a viaduct across the Mawddach between Fairbourne and Barmouth, and commenced another across the mouth of the Dyfi from Ynyslas to Aberdyfi. This latter proved to be a 'bridge too far', which together with his nucleus of a seaside town at Ynyslas subsiding into the sand, precipitated Savin's insolvency in 1866.

In spite of their own rocky finances, the Cambrian Railways took on the Savin lines, with David Davies overseeing work on the uncompleted sections. This was not because of any enthusiasm for Savin's fancy hotel ideas nor because there was any real desire to reach Porth Dinllaen, but rather to reach the Gwynedd slate and, more importantly, to forestall the G.W.R.'s ideas of doing so.

At Ynyslas the building of the viaduct was abandoned, as was the idea of developing the temporary wharfage at the mouth of the river Leri into a floating dock. To provide a crossing of the Dyfi a branch line, the Morben Railway was built, leaving the Machynlleth-Aberystwyth line at Morben Junction (later Dovey Junction), 4 miles south of Machynlleth, crossing the Dyfi by a relatively modest 140 yard bridge. Then as the Mindovey Railway, it continued along the northern bank of the river to arrive at Aberdyfi in 1867, requiring some rather heavy engineering, including four tunnels, to do so. There it made an end-on junction with the Aberdyfi-Fairbourne section, with a spur to Aberdyfi harbour.

This final piece in the southern part of what is now the Cambrian Coast Line was of great slate significance. To build the Machynlleth-Aberystwyth line the river had been diverted at Derwenlas leaving the little port literally high and dry. Therefore slate coming down the tramway from Corris was forced to load onto the railway at Machynlleth. This, together with slate brought down the Mawddwy Railway could now be railed direct to Aberdyfi harbour. These shipments added to the Talyllyn tonnages, boosted Aberdyfi's shipments as well as rekindling interest in slate quarrying around Aberdyfi itself at diggings such as Alltgoch (SH620964). The lower end of the Corris Tramway having thus fallen into disuse was officially abandoned in 1878.

In anticipation of the railway crossing the Dyfi, plans had been drawn up to enlarge Aberdyfi harbour, including a substantial floating dock, but although trade did grow during the late 1860s, it was never enough to justify really big expenditure. By 1882 when a new wooden jetty was opened, the depression and increasing rail distribution, had begun the Aberdyfi slate trade's slide into what became oblivion during WW1.

Meanwhile in 1865 the line north from Aberdyfi and Tywyn reached Fairbourne on the south side of the Mawddach estuary. From there (then known as Barmouth Ferry station) passengers for Barmouth and beyond could, pending the completion of the bridge, take the horse bus to the ferry at Penrhyn point. The line continued up the south bank of the estuary, coming to a halt in the middle of nowhere at Penmaenpool, effectively discouraging the G.W.R.–sponsored Ruabon-Dolgellau line from venturing west of Dolgellau. Any lingering aspirations the G.W.R. may still have had being killed in 1869 when the Cambrian extended from Penmaenpool to make an end-on junction at Dolgellau.

It was not until 1867 that trains could cross the Barmouth viaduct, curiously trains were allowed on the viaduct from 5th July but locomotives were not, so until 9th October carriages were drawn over the viaduct by horses. By the end of the year the line north of Barmouth was open to Porthmadog, within sight of but not yet within reach of, the 'Blaenau Bonanza'.

As has been said Savin had threatened to build a branch to Blaenau. This proved an empty gesture but his Beddgelert Railway was not, and in 1865 he began this 9 mile standard gauge branch from west of the proposed site of A. & W.C.R. Porthmadog station intending to reach Beddgelert via the west bank of the Glaslyn river. There was to be a branch at SH593436 to run up the east side of the Aberglaslyn pass via a 297 yard tunnel to Pont Bethania to serve Hafod y Llan quarry (SH613524), the one substantial quarry in the Beddgelert area which a somewhat speculative report of 1869 claimed, 'might support 60 bargains', (i.e. about 300 men). Savin's 1866 financial problems stopped work on the branch with just some formations part-built.

Also never built was the A. & W.C.R. scheme to re-site the Glaslyn sluices much further upstream near their bridge at Y Garth, and to build two levees to create a triangle of tidal water along the full length of the landward side of the Cob which would be widened to provide several hundred yards of quay, accessible by making the Britannia bridge openable. The cob wharfage would have been connected to the main line by a branch to the east of Porthmadog station.

It was in anticipation of this inner harbour that in 1862 the brothers M and J Roberts build their flour mill at what was expected to be a wharf. In the event they had to bring grain, from the quayside by a shuttle service of two horses pulling three 2 ton wagons over the Croesor tramway tracks.

What was built in 1868, was the Beddgelert siding, a short spur on the formation of Savin's intended Beddgelert branch, and having exchange facilities with the Croesor Tramway which closely paralleled it.

No big deal in itself, since it was obvious that slate tonnages coming down the Croesor would never be substantial. However since the Croesor and the F.R. shared metals at Porthmadog quays, traffic coming down the F.R. could be worked back along the Croesor to the interchange. Thus Blaenau slate could now be dispatched over the national rail network, bringing to over 90%, the proportion of Welsh slate able to be distributed by rail. This Beddgelert siding exchange also acted as a link between the railway and the port via the Croesor tracks and also enabled the Porthmadog flour mill to deliver by rail.

The effect of rail connection on this upstart town of Porthmadog would prove to be dramatic. Already an important port and ship building centre with half a dozen shipyards, from now on its foundries, slate merchants and finishers, Building Societies and Insurance Companies would dominate the economy of southern Caernarfonshire and northern Meirionnydd.

The Cambrian of course never reached Porth Dinllaen nor St. Tudwalls south of Abersoch which the A. & W.C. had seen as a potential embarkation point for Ireland. It did eventually reach Pwllheli (about ½ mile short of the present station which was not opened until 1909), all but bankrupting itself in the process. Curiously, in 1884 with the glory days of slate over and steamships spelling the end of little local harbours, Porth Dinllaen was the subject of one last nostalgic bid, the Portdinlaen Railway. Fortunately for its sponsors, this westward extension from Pwllheli which would have involved much engineering including tunnels of 283 and 220 yards plus extensive harbour works, failed to find support.

The railway-influenced growth of Porthmadog into a Regional Capital was to some extent at Pwllheli's expense and although its record of 400 ships built was never reached by any other Caernarfonshire port, this and related trades declined there from the late 1860s.

Besides Blaenau output, the A. & W.C.R. also found some slate pickings along the way. The little diggings at Harlech (SH572304 – 578308) may have used the railway and Llanfair quarry (SH580288) and the small quarries in the hinterland dispatched some output via Pensarn station instead of using Pensarn wharf. Further south, Tyddyn Sieffre abandoned its wharf and turned its tramway to meet a siding on the Barmouth junction triangle near Barmouth Junction (later Morfa Mawddach) station. Arthog quarry relaid its incline to a siding on the Barmouth Junction-Penmaenpool section, although in both cases tonnages were small. More fruitful were the developments at Henddol (SH619122) and Goelwern (SH621122) quarries. Having previously been able to ferry only trifling quantities to Barmouth, they could now load onto the railway at Fairbourne. Although their planned tramway there was never built, useful tonnages were carted, an excellent example of how economic potential could be unlocked by the availability of rail transport.

The Cambrian may have distanced itself from Savin's grandiose hotels, but the completion of the coastal line attracted independent developers and populations of towns along the route typically doubled in little more than a decade. This in turn had a further rail association. Solomon Andrews of Cardiff used a 3' 6" tramway to assist his building activities on the western side of Pwllheli, subsequently relaid as a horse-drawn passenger tramway extending 4 miles to Llanbedrog, these being the only rails ever to run beyond Pwllheli and the nearest any ever got to Porth Dinllaen. Similarly when the 2' Tyddyn Sieffre line became disused, Andrews adopted it to serve his less successful housing development to the east of the southern end of the Barmouth viaduct. In the same area MacDougalls, of flour fame laid rails at Fairbourne for the same purpose, the formation of which was later used by the Fairbourne Miniature Railway.

7 The 1860s. The rest of Wales

In Dyffryn Conwy, in the north of Gwynedd, slate was still being shipped down river to Conwy. Some was loaded from wharves on either side of the river at the old Roman ford at Tal-y-cafn, but most was put on board at Trefriw, where a new wharf had been built in 1835.

Even before the Chester & Holyhead Railway reached Conwy in 1848, the possibility of a feeder line to bring slate (and lead, sulphur & pyrites) from the mines and quarries up valley had been discussed. The first firm proposal was the Conway & Llanrwst Railway of 1853 which envisaged a 3' gauge, locomotive powered line from an exchange station at Conwy to run along the western side of the valley, crossing to the east just north of Llanrwst. Branches would serve mines in the Gwydir forest and the slate workings in Cwm Eigiau. A horse-drawn extension to Betws-y-coed would split three ways to serve Hafodlas quarry (SH779562), the various quarries at Dolwyddelan and those in the Machno valley.

Nothing but talk ensued for almost five years, when a simplified plan, the 3' 3" Conway & Llanrwst Railway was submitted, backed by H.B. Roberts (of Croesor Tramway fame).

In 1860 the L. & N.W.R. having taken over the running of the C. & H. put a stop to these local ideas by sponsoring a standard gauge branch up the east side of the valley from what was to become Llandudno Junction.

Although this new Conway & Llanrwst Railway had neither plans nor authorisation to go beyond Llanrwst, William Dew a partner in Hafodlas quarry wrote in 1862, – 'there is no question that it (the railway) will shortly be extended to pass the foot of our incline'. That same year, and presumably with the same expectations, Foel quarry (SH717556) constructed the fine **Moel Siabod Tramway**. Of

2' gauge and 1½ miles long, it left the quarry by an incline from the foot of which it ran by gravity (with horse return) to the head of an incline system of one long shallow pitch and two shorter, steep pitches, to reach the road at Pont Cyfyng about 800' below. Shortly after opening, the lowest pitch was extended to a riverside mill. (From 1874 it also carried output from Rhos quarry [SH729564] by way of a feeder which joined part way down the long incline.)

It was 1863 before the C. & L. reached Llanrwst, remaining there well short of Betws and its contributory valleys. There were of course slate quarries in the Llanrwst area, but a railway on the east bank of the river was of limited value to them, since most were in hanging valleys to the west. In 1861 the newly re-opened Cedryn quarry (SH719635), high in the vastnesses of Carnedd Llywelyn, realising that the commencement of the east side line ended any hopes of a railway on the western side, built the **Cedryn Tramway**.

Of 2' gauge and 4 miles long, horse/gravity worked, it began at the foot of a cart road (or possibly an incline) from the quarry. It followed a gentle down grade for 1¾ miles, where at the end of a stone embankment it dropped to ground level by the short Pwll Du incline. From there it continued for 1¼ miles to the lip of the hanging valley. The Conwy valley some 850' below was reached by a three pitch incline, the two upper pitches end on, the lowest turning slightly northward to dive under the road. From there a ½ mile run across the Conwy flood plain took it to a wharf on the river at Porth Llwyd. (This final part of the line was relaid during the 1906/7 construction of the Aluminium works as a temporary tramway.)

By about 1864, there was a ¾ mile extension which took the line up the far side of the Eigiau valley to Cwm Eigiau quarry (SH702635). This extension also served a new Cedryn mill which due to water constraints had to be remotely sited and connected to the quarry by a viaduct.

In the meantime the C. & L. remained terminated at Llanrwst, much to the benefit of this relatively important agricultural centre, but with little prospect of worthwhile freight revenues. It was only after almost five years that it was extended to Betws-y-coed as the Llandudno Junction to Betws y Coed branch, opening for goods in 1867 and passengers in 1868. This line now wholly owned by the London & North Western, served no slate quarries along its route since with the exception of Cefn Madoc (SH825654), the diggings to the east of the Conwy valley were tiny, mainly producing a coarse block used locally for building.

However at Betws-y-coed itself it was in a position to pick up substantial slate traffic from quarries such as Cwm Machno (SH751470), Foel/Rhos, Hafodlas and the Lledr valley workings around Dolwyddelan, shortening their cartages and avoiding the congestion at Trefriw and at Tal-y-cafn where the wharf had become so crowded that Cwm Machno quarry had to stockpile product awaiting shipment eight miles away near Betws. Since the facilities at Conwy Town Quay were somewhat exiguous and were not rail connected a new St. George's pier and harbour at Deganwy was opened in 1868, served by a spur from the Llandudno branch of the L. & N.W.R.

Slate apart, the Betws connection made the town a focus for the Lledr, Llugwy, Machno and upper Conwy valleys and a centre for the lead mining of the Gwydir Forest. Passenger services, apart from ending the isolation of Betws also opened it up as an important tourist town.

On the west bank of the Conwy there were, besides the Cedryn and Cwm Eigiau quarries, perhaps half a dozen slate sites as well as metal mines, shipping at Trefriw, additionally Trefriw, with its sulphur springs, had tourist ambitions. Accordingly in the late 1870s there was a proposal for a narrow gauge rail connection from Llanrwst station to Trefriw, but the slate trade recession put a stop to

RAILS TO CAERNARFON
1869

SINCE 1867 THE CARNAVONSHIRE RAILWAY TO AFON WEN HAS PARTLY SUBSUMED THE NANTLLE TRAMWAY. PENDING THE CONVERSION OF THE PORT LINES TO STANDARD GAUGE IN 1872, TRAFFIC FOR THE PORT HAS TO BE TRANSFERRED AT PANT.

THE LLANBERIS BRANCH HAS JUST OPENED ENCOURAGING THE DEVELOPMENT OF QUARRIES THERE BUT, FOR THE TIME BEING AT LEAST, THE LAYOUT DOES NOT FAVOUR THEIR USING THE PORT.

the plan. It is, incidentally, possible that the later Gower footbridge (SH792622) and its approach paths defined the line of the southern part of this scheme. When in 1907 a standard gauge branch crossed the river to serve the Aluminium works at Dolgarrog, it was suggested that an electric tramway could use the bridge to link a new station on the L. & N.W.R. with Trefriw. This idea was revived in 1910, but was superseded by the Conway Valley Light Railway proposal which was a standard gauge edition of the Conwy-Llanrwst part of Roberts' 1868 west bank line. By the time the C.V.L.R. plan was finally abandoned post WW1, serious slate working and most other industry in Dyffryn Conwy was history.

Over in the north west, the Nantlle Railway had been leased by Edward Preston who, in about 1856, commenced a timetabled passenger service offering first, second and third class travel. The Caernarfon to Talysarn journey took 1½ hours, but with fares about in line with those of the steam railways, it did provide the thriving Penygroes/Talysarn area with comparatively cheap communication with Caernarfon. To keep to timetable, the horses had to maintain a brisk pace, so 'fast' passenger trains mixed up with slate runs were an obvious source of problems.

From the early 1850s there had been several plans to extend or supplant the Nantlle. In fact in 1852 even before the Bangor & Caernarfon Railway was completed, the Carnarvon & Portmadoc Railway had been promoted. An alternative proposal involved a branch of the Nantlle meeting the standard gauge at Caernarfon town station, and an extension to the Drws y Coed copper mines and on to the slate quarries in Cwm Gwyrfai. At the same time there were rival schemes to outflank the Nantlle such as the Llynfi Vale Railway and Harbour proposal of 1858 which would have connected Talysarn with a new harbour at Pontllyfni. More ambitious was the proposal confusingly titled 'Nantlle

Railway', which was for a line from Caernarfon town station, curving round the south of Penygroes and swinging north to the west of Llyn Nantlle Uchaf. There were also various suggestions for extending south to Porthmadog, Pwllheli and even continuing from there to the old favourite, Porth Dinllaen. At the same time there was talk that when the proposed Aberystwyth & Welch Coast got beyond Porthmadog, it would send a branch north to Penygroes to siphon off Nantlle traffic, an idea viewed with askance at Caernarfon.

This latter was countered in 1862 by the Carnarvonshire Railway proposal, which was a re-vamp of the C. & P.R. of ten years before, backed by some local landowners, Blaenau quarry proprietors Holland, Matthew, Greaves and Casson, as well as Preston himself. It was intended to tap the Ffestiniog potential by extending the standard gauge from Caernarfon town to beat the Aberystwyth & Welch Coast to Porthmadog by crossing the mouth of the Seiont (as the 1850s Bangor-Porth Dinllaen line had intended to do) and, run roughly parallel to the Caernarfon-Porthmadog road. A branch to serve Pwllheli would leave near Garn Dolbenmaen. Most oddly Thomas Savin then the driving force behind the A. & W.C.R. was deeply involved in this plan. Never a man to 'let his left hand know what his right hand was doing', Savin may either have been hedging his bets or was in cahoots with the L. & N.W.R., with ideas of forming a ring around Snowdonia to keep the G.W.R. out.

By 1864 this scheme had become the ambitious Carnarvon, Penygroes & Pwllheli Direct Railway. It was to run end on from Caernarfon station, tunnel under Castle Square, cross and re-cross the Nantlle Railway and run south to the east of it roughly along the line of the main road, crossing near Groeslon to follow east of the Pwllheli road to near Four Crosses where it would swing east to join the proposed A. & W.C.R. line from Porthmadog to Pwllheli. A branch would leave immediately south of Caernarfon, crossing and re-crossing the Seiont several times, reaching the Gwyrfai near Waunfawr it would run up the north side of the valley. At Rhyd Ddu it would cross to the south of the road, drop down to Beddgelert where it would cross the Glaslyn and keeping to the east of the river join the A. & W.C.R. just west of Porthmadog station. Another branch would leave at Penygroes and after passing well to the south of Talysarn, would turn north to terminate at Nantlle village, where it would pick up traffic from a short eastward extension of the Nantlle Railway at an exchange station.

In the end what did open in 1867 was the **Carnarvon-Afon Wen Branch**. At first it started from Pant just south of Caernarfon running due south to join the Cambrian/A. & W.C.R. at Afon Wen, about two miles east of where the C.P. & P.D. has hoped to join it. A year later, the 167 yard tunnel under the town was completed enabling an end-on junction with the Bangor-Caernarfon line at Caernarfon station.

This Caernarfon-Afon Wen line was viewed with some consternation by the good Burgesses of Caernarfon. Not only did it facilitate the distribution of Nantlle valley slate by rail, but it offered the possibility for it to go south for shipment at Porthmadog. Little if any did go south, but of course output increasingly went by rail. However although the line contributed to Caernarfon's decline as a port it most valuably linked Caernarfon and Bangor with Pwllheli, Porthmadog and Meirionnydd. It also provided an improved service to Llanwnda, Groeslon, Penygroes and Llanllyfni and the stations at Pant Glas, Bryncir, Ynys, Llangybi and Chwilog brought the isolated Pwllheli/Cricieth hinterland within the ambit of Caernarfon.

However all this was bad news for the Nantlle's quarry customers since with arrogant disregard for their requirements, it had hi-jacked the trackbed of the Nantlle tramway from Coed Helen south of Caernarfon, to Tyddyn Bengam (SH472544), just north of Penygroes. This meant that up to a hundred Nantlle wagons having to be loaded onto transporters at Tyddyn Bengam each day, then unloaded at Pant (SH483616), to be horse drawn to the Caernarfon slate quays. Additionally empty wagons and return loads including 100 tons per week of quarry coal had to be similarly handled. Such were the delays that some quarries reverted to carts. Unlike the Padarn where four quarry wagons were carried longitudinally, the Nantlle wagons, being wider had to be carried in threes transversely. This caused difficulties where overhanging loads such as long slate slabs, timbers, pipes etc. were carried.

This state of affairs clearly could not be allowed to continue but what to do about it was hotly debated. There could be little argument that a consistent gauge was called for, preferably locomotive worked. This could be either by relaying the remaining 3' 6" route in heavier track, and third-railing the standard gauge between Tyddyn Bengam and Pant, or alternatively relaying everything in standard gauge. The latter at least was a non-starter since east of Talysarn the Nantlle trackbed was subject to repeated re-alignments due to encroachment by quarry workings and there were fears that the vibration of full-sized locomotives would initiate rock falls in the quarries.

There were ideas of making a standard gauge branch from Penygroes to Talysarn and converting the line east of Talysarn and on the Caernarfon quays to 2' gauge. This gauge could then be standardised throughout the quarries and would result in wagons which would be more readily carried by transporter. It was even suggested that the standard gauge be ignored altogether and 2' gauge metals be run right through to Caernarfon quays on a totally new formation. This latter notion would have been welcomed in Caernarfon since it would effectively keep Nantlle slate off the main line and direct it on to Caernarfon ships.

Matters were resolved in 1872 when a sub-branch was made to Talysarn from the Caernarfon-Afon Wen line immediately south of Penygroes, partly on the Nantlle trackbed. Exchange sidings at Talysarn served the quarries on the northern side of the vale via the remaining rump of the Nantlle with, from 1881, the adjacent Coed Madog quarry (SH490530) having its own standard gauge connection.

Simultaneously the Caernarfon slate quays were relaid as standard gauge, which besides the obvious slate handling advantages, gave railway connection to De Winton's Union Foundry, Owen Jones' slate works and the town gas works. There was a further idea of extending the standard gauge from Talysarn to Nantlle village by a line (the Talysarn Railway), looping round south to Nantlle village, apparently to outflank the remaining rump of the Nantlle tramway. Oddly, a variation of this rather curious proposal was unsuccessfully revived in 1889 as the Talysarn Junction Railway.

A siding (the Tanyrallt siding) between Penygroes and Talysarn served the Caernarvonshire Slate Quarries Railway, which continued as a 3' 6" horse-drawn tramway.

Although the taking over by the Standard Gauge of routes pioneered by horse tramways was commonplace in coal mining areas, this Caernarfon-Talysarn route was a unique example in north west Wales.

Although slate shipments from Caernarfon continued to be buoyant for the time being, the Talysarn line encouraged inland rail distribution and even the 1878 completion of the fine Victoria dock could not stem the decline of Caernarfon's maritime slate trade.

None of the proposed extensions of the Nantlle tramway was ever built but in 1868 its scope was extended by the 1½ mile, 3' 6" gauge **John Robinson Tramway**. This arose from the 1864 development of Fron quarry (SH515548) by the British Slate Co. (later Carnarvon & Bangor Slate Co.), under its energetic Managing Director, John Robinson and its amalgamation with Old Braich (SH512549). Since these quarries were located on a remote but potentially slate-rich area, a rail link to Caernarfon was immediately planned. Daunted by the cost, what was actually built was a tramway past the top of Cilgwyn quarry (SH500540) enabling traffic to reach the Nantlle tramway via Talysarn Quarry (SH496534), also being owned by the C. & B.S.C. Almost immediately Braich quarry (SH510552), having been taken over by a new partnership which included the 'rail minded' H.B. Roberts, made a connection to it. There is a record of the line being described as 'capable of being loco worked', but it seems unlikely that any were used, since part of the deal with Braich was that they should supply horses.

Though comparatively unimportant in itself, this line was the first to provide rail transport to the abundant but hitherto isolated slate of the Moel Tryfan area.

By the late 1860s the only slate diggings of note which lacked rail connection of any kind were those on Cefn Ddu to the south west of Llyn Padarn. An attempt had been made to remedy this in 1864 with the Bangor and Llanberis Direct Railway. This curious private line would have left the L. & N.W.R. immediately west of Bangor Station and would have begun by running parallel to and inland of the railway to Caernarfon. Undaunted by the gradients involved it would have climbed inland before dropping down around the western end of Llyn Padarn to reach Llanberis. A more sensible route, from immediately east of Caernarfon station was looked at, but the opening of the Caernarfon-Afon Wen line enabled the branch to be taken up the Seiont valley from south of Caernarfon. This the L. & N.W.R. **Llanberis branch** opened in 1869, its 9 mile route beginning at Pant almost opposite the slate quays junction.

It transformed the fortunes of almost a dozen quarries which had been working excellent and abundant slate but had been handicapped by having to cart to Caernarfon.

Sidings were laid to give Glynrhonwy Lower (SH565607) direct access and Goodman's (SH572606) could reach it by its pre-existing tramway. By c.1874 almost all the eight or nine quarries higher up the hill, could reach the railway by the remarkable 1000 yard Ffridd Incline.

This magnificent incline was single acting, empties being uphauled by a 14hp De Winton steam winder. A conventional self-acting gravity system could not be used since the weight of rope limited such inclines to pitches of around 600-700 yards, and friction in a layout of this length would make an endless rope arrangement out of the question. From the head of this main pitch a further three self-acting tandem pitches of 265, 300 & 260 yards connected with the summit quarries such as Chwarel Fawr (SH552600) and Bwlch y Groes (SH560600) almost 1200' above. Most of the quarries later amalgamated, but the setting up of this incline system under diverse ownership was a remarkable example of co-operation.

Unfortunately for Caernarfon the Slate Quays were not directly accessible by standard gauge until 1872, by which time the use of Deganwy as a shipping point for this Llanberis material was well established. In any case heavy use of the branch was to prove short-lived, since most of the Llanberis quarries fared very badly after the 1877 collapse of the slate market.

However the line provided a lasting link to the Seiont brickworks and to Griffith Robert's Glanmorfa writing slate works, just outside Caernarfon, it also served the Peblig flour mill and the Peblig brickworks as well as the Jones slate works situated between the S.G. line and the Padarn Railway at Pont Rhythallt. Such a location offered the slate works a choice both of raw material source and of dispatch route, enabling it to expand eastwards into a substantial multiple site.

Besides the usual gains to Llanberis of having rail connection, it gave a considerable fillip to tourism resulting in the development of a substantial hotel trade. The fact that the catchment at the intermediate stations at Pont Rhug, Pontrhythallt and Cwm-y-glo was relatively numerous, also augmented the line's passenger traffic.

This branch could have been even more useful had a planned sub-branch, the Carnarvon & Llandwrog Railway been built. It would have left the Llanberis branch 1½ miles from Caernarfon and run south to Fron quarry, thus properly opening up the Moel Tryfan area in a way that John Robinson line never could. A proposed spur to Cilgwyn would have spared that quarry the clanking uncertainties of the Nantlle tramway and another sub-branch at Llanrug could have served the Gwyrfai valley.

By the end of the 1860s the standard gauge network in mid and north Wales was all but complete, with connections which potentially enabled almost all the Welsh slate output to make use of it. Indeed the decade had seen the opening of two lines, the Mawddwy and the Talyllyn, which directed their respective quarries' output exclusively onto main line railways, indicating that rail was fast becoming the preferred method of inland distribution.

However there was one tramway desperately seeking a railway to hook onto. Mention has been made of the Hafod y Llan quarry (SH613524), in a hanging valley high on the southern slopes of Snowdon, carting to the Croesor Tramway. As early as 1843 the success of the Nantlle and the F.R. had prompted ideas of Hafod y Llan quarry building a tramway to Porthmadog, which could also have served the Sygun copper mine, then under common ownership. This was dropped when it was realised that outputs did not justify the cost which would have been £1500-2000 per mile, plus costs of land, plus heavy legal fees if a Parliamentary Act was required in order to compulsory acquire land. Nevertheless this scheme was revived c.1858 and by 1862 it had become the Snowdon and Portmadoc Railway, a 2' gauge steam hauled passenger line, which had it been built might have predated the steamed F.R. These ideas were dropped in 1865 when their main proponent, Alan Searell manager of Hafod y Llan died, and in any case with work then starting at Porthmadog on the Beddgelert Railway, it seemed Hafod y Llan no longer needed to build a line themselves, but with this apparently imminent prospect of a full-scale standard gauge railway running along Nant Gwynant, a link to it became a priority.

At the time, finished output from the Hafod y Llan mill was taken by a short tramway to a cart loading point, from where it set out on a perilous journey down copper mine tracks to the valley floor at Pont Bethania some 1000' below. This was replaced by the truly heroic **South Snowdon Tramway**. Of 2' gauge and 1½ miles long, extensive civil work enabled it to follow a gentle down slope for almost a mile after which a spectacular incline, shortly followed by a second more modest one absorbed much of the 1000' fall of the line to the valley floor. Horses were apparently used on the upper stretch but between the inclines trucks may have been manhandled. Before the line was completed in 1868, work on the Beddgelert Railway had ceased, but construction pressed ahead confident that someone would build a line of some kind.

Like Foel and Rhos at Capel Curig and Hafodlas at Betws-y-coed, they would wait in vain for a railway, and their temporary expedient of carting to the Croesor Tramway at Pont Portreuddyn would become permanent.

In the same year an economically insignificant, but vitally portentous line was opened in the south of Meirionnydd. This, the 3' gauge (later 2') **Cwm Ebol Tramway** ran from Cwm Ebol quarry (SH689017), for 1½ miles, via two self-acting inclines to Llyn Bwtri, the traditional shipping point on the Dyfi for the Bryneglwys/Cantrebedd quarries. For a time this little line also served a quartz mine, an example of how a slate railway could enable an otherwise unviable enterprise to succeed. This classic quarry/shipping point layout, adopted because the railway was on the opposite bank of the river, made Cwm Ebol the last Welsh slate quarry to be connected to a shipping point rather than to a main line railway.

Although it would be almost exactly a century before the last slates were dispatched from a Welsh port (Port Dinorwig 1969), from now on the extinction of Welsh slate shipping was inevitable.

Manod Viaduct. Ffestiniog & Blaenau Railway 1870s.
(Courtesy National Library of Wales)

The Harbour, Aberdyfi 1870s.
(Courtesy National Library of Wales)

Tal-y-cafn Ferry, slate wharf on east bank of the Conwy. 1890s
(Courtesy National Library of Wales)

Port Dinorwig. Standard Gauge entering from centre, Narrow Gauge from right.
(Courtesy National Library of Wales)

Padarn Railway, slate wagons on transporter.
(Courtesy National Library of Wales)

GWR, Blaenau station, slate wagons on transporter for return to Graig Ddu.
(Courtesy National Library of Wales)

Ex G.W.R., Tan y Manod. LH line branch to engine shed, turntable and Graig Ddu exchange. RH line is running line to Llan Ffestiniog and Bala. 1961. (Courtesy Michael Hale Esq.)

Ex G.W.R., Blaenau station, looking west. LH line is F.R. connection to the S.G./N.G. exchange sidings (also previously to Newborough slate factory). Central line is the S.G. headshunt. RH line is the F.R. Duffws branch. 1959 (Courtesy Michael Hale Esq.)

Dyfi Bridge, Corris Railway.
(Courtesy National Library of Wales)

Machynlleth Station, Corris Railway.
(Courtesy National Library of Wales)

Ffestiniog Railway, Little Wonder at Porthmadog c.1880.
(Courtesy National Library of Wales)

Glyn Valley Tramway.
(Courtesy National Library of Wales)

Pont Fawr, Blaenau Ffestiniog. Carried Oakeley quarry material to Glan y Don Tip and mill, over Ffestiniog Railway Dinas branch and L.&N.W.R. (L.M.S.R.) Blaenau branch. (Courtesy G.R. Jones Esq.)

G.W.R. Bala-Blaenau branch, spur at Manod to Madog roadstone quarry. (Courtesy G.R. Jones Esq.)

Tal-y-llyn Railway Abergynolwyn station.
(Courtesy Royal Commission on Ancient & Historic Monuments in Wales)

Welsh Highland Railway, Porthmadog 'New' station.
(Courtesy Royal Commission on Ancient & Historic Monuments in Wales)

Dinorwig Tramway underpass. 1980.
(Photo - Author)

Padarn Railway, Penscoins drumhouse. 1984.
(Photo - Author)

Penrhyn Railroad, lane defines route at Llandegai. 1984.
(Photo - Author)

Blaenau station. S.G. tracks on L occupy site of old F.R. lines. The blank road
approximately defines old headshunt. N.G. line follows route of F.R. lines to
exchange sidings and to Newborough Slate Works. 2000.
(Photo - Author)

Ex N.W.N.G., ex W.H.R. Russell at W.H.R. (1964) station. 2000.
(Photo - Author)

F.R. Taliesin heads double Fairlie David Lloyd George at F.R. Harbour station. 2000.
(Photo - Author)

F.R./W.H.R. Mountaineer at Dinas station. 2000.
(Photo - Author)

F.R. Blanche at Minffordd. 2000.
(Photo - Author)

Tal-y-llyn Railway. Dolgoch at Wharf station. 2000.
(Photo - Author)

Nantlle Tramway, Bontnewydd. 1988.
(Photo - Author)

Ex-L.&N.W.R. at tunnel portal, Blaenau. To L on site of Llechwedd exchange sidings, sheds and crane, also Llechwedd power station. Centre site of Glanydon tip. R of line site of Oakeley exchange sidings and pillar of Penybont viaduct. 2000.
(Photo - Author)

Deeside Tramway, wooden rails on ground. 1986.
(Photo - Author)

Embankment of South Snowdon tramway cuts steep route of old copper mine tramway. 1980.
(Photo - Author)

John Robinson Tramway runs between walls of smallholdings. 2000.
(Photo - Author)

111

*F.R. Stesion Fain, Blaenau. Canopy in reuse as stand for
Manod Football Club. 2000.
(Photo - Author)*

*Croesor Tramway, Blaen y Cwm bridge. 1976.
(Photo - Author)*

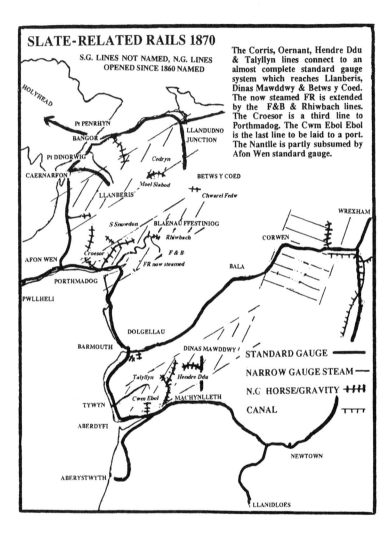

SLATE-RELATED RAILS 1870

S.G. LINES NOT NAMED, N.G. LINES
OPENED SINCE 1860 NAMED

The Corris, Oernant, Hendre Ddu & Talyllyn lines connect to an almost complete standard gauge system which reaches Llanberis, Dinas Mawddwy & Betws y Coed. The now steamed FR is extended by the F&B & Rhiwbach lines. The Croesor is a third line to Porthmadog. The Cwm Ebol Ebol is the last line to be laid to a port. The Nantile is partly subsumed by Afon Wen standard gauge.

HOLYHEAD

Pt PENRHYN
BANGOR
LLANDUDNO
JUNCTION

Pt DINORWIG
Cedryn

CAERNARFON
BETWS Y COED
Moel Siabod

LLANBERIS
Chwarel Fedw

WREXHAM

S Snowdon
BLAENAU FFESTINIOG
Rhiwbach
CORWEN

Croesor
F & B
FR now steamed

AFON WEN
BALA

PORTHMADOG

PWLLHELI

DOLGELLAU

BARMOUTH
DINAS MAWDDWY

STANDARD GAUGE ——

NARROW GAUGE STEAM —

Talyllyn   Hendre Ddu

N.G HORSE/GRAVITY ┼┼┼

TYWYN
Cwm Ebol   MACHYNLLETH

CANAL ⊤⊤⊤

ABERDYFI

NEWTOWN

ABERYSTWYTH

LLANIDLOES

114

8 The 1870s. Boom and Bust

The Standard Gauge & feeders

The 1870s opened with slate outputs, prices and prospects of prosperity climbing to even dizzier heights with no one imagining that before the decade was out the bubble would burst and the industry would begin a hundred years of almost continuous decline. By mid-decade with prices advancing 10% or more per annum and the quarries months in arrears with their deliveries, such a catastrophe was unimaginable and everyone, particularly the rail companies, were desperate to grab a 'piece of the action'.

The greatest expansion in output was at Blaenau Ffestiniog, where the Ffestiniog Railway's traffic had been augmented by new connections such as the spur to the foot of the dizzy Nyth y Gigfran (SH689462) incline and the Cwm Orthin tramway extension to Conglog quarry (SH668467), increasing its quarry connections to sixteen.

F.R. slate traffic could of course reach the Cambrian Railways via the Beddgelert siding and in spite of this calling for the trundling of trucks through the back streets of Porthmadog and the paying of dues both to the harbour and the Croesor, by the early 1870s the Cambrian's share of F.R. traffic approached 10%. So great was the increase in Blaenau production, that this percentage was scarcely missed at the Porthmadog wharves.

In 1872 matters dramatically changed with the opening of the Minffordd Exchange, which enabled Ffestiniog Railway traffic to be transferred directly onto the Cambrian Railways. Minffordd's excellent facilities and convenience immediately resulted in an increasing proportion of F.R. traffic failing to even reach Porthmadog, let alone be shipped there. In contrast with the first main line connections made at Port Penrhyn and Port Dinorwig twenty years earlier, the railways could now offer connection with almost every part of Britain. Besides which, not only had rail rates fallen, but in the boom times of the early 1870s costs were less important than speed of delivery.

This, followed by the fall in slate production in the late 1870s, sent a chill wind through both port and town, as slate shipments to British destinations began lapsing into oblivion. Although Porthmadog, with its substantial export trade fared better than some other slate ports, within less than a decade its shipbuilding had all but ceased. For this the railways were not to blame as by 1880 it was costing at least £22 per ton to build a wooden sailing ship in Wales, whereas Canadian vessels were coming onto the market at under £20. The recovery in the slate trade during the 1890s did revive Porthmadog shipbuilding, but sadly this revival, like the upturn in the slate trade proved very temporary.

The Minffordd interchange also robbed Porthmadog of imports by encouraging general supplies for Blaenau to come in by rail. Besides which its coal tipper could fill F.R. trucks many times faster than hauling it out of coastwise vessels. The Minffordd exchange was also a valuable passenger facility, obviating the trek from one end of Porthmadog to the other to transfer from the F.R. to the Cambrian.

Over on the other side of northern Wales, in a much more modest way, the G.W.R. Ruabon-Dolgellau line was also increasing its share of slate traffic thanks to the mid 1870s development of the Deeside (SJ138404) and the Moelfferna (SJ125399) quarries. Against the trend, tonnages, particularly from Moelfferna, held up well following the slump, partly due to their product being predominately slab, which was less seriously affected by the downturn than roofing slate, and partly because their proximity to England saved a vital few pennies per ton on carriage.

Whilst the slate potential of the Dee valley exercised no influence in the decision to build a railway along it, this was an example of a railway's presence enabling slate to be successfully worked at places where it might otherwise have been unprofitable.

Ouput from these quarries was carried to the main line by a most unusual means, the 2' 6" gauge, wooden railed **Deeside Tramway**. This line originally connected Deeside quarry with the main road at Glyndyfrdwy by way of the Nant y Pandy mill (SJ148417) so sited to obtain water power for sawing slate blocks.

The line was extended south in iron rail up to Moelfferna in the late 1870s, and at about the same time, north to Glyndyfrdwy station, doubling its length to almost 3 miles. Whilst the date of original opening is disputed, it is certainly not earlier than the 1850s by which time the use of wooden rails sheathed in iron is bizarre. The unusual gauge may have been due to coal mining influences.

The Deeside's all-gravity working of loads was not in trains but in individual trucks. All down working was left to the end of the day so providing a free ride home for workmen perching on wagons operating the brakes. The empties were returned in horse-drawn trains each morning.

Apart from quarry supplies which latterly included oil fuel for Moelfferna, no goods were carried, nor was there ever provision for, nor indeed need of, passenger facilities to this desolate spot.

Not quite such an oddity, but also anachronistic was the **Glyn Valley Tramway** of 1873. Apart from being horse drawn, it deliberately avoided contact with a main line railway.

Built at the instigation of the Cambrian quarry (SJ189378), it was partly financed by the Montgomeryshire Canal Company then owned by the L. & N.W.R., who were clearly determined to prevent its lucrative mineral traffic, finding its way onto the G.W.R. Shrewsbury to Wrexham line.

It ran from Glynceiriog to the canal at Chirk Bank, partly as a roadside line and partly via the bed of a disused colliery tramway, carefully bridging the G.W.R. en route. Apart from the climb up to and across the railway, the moderate gradient was with the load and thus could be partially gravity worked with the horse riding in the old F.R. manner. Its unusual gauge of a 'half standard' 2' 4¼" conformed to the ruling quarry gauge in the area. Between 1874 and 1886 passengers were carried on the Glynceiriog-Pontfaen roadside section, although they occasionally found themselves riding in empty slate trucks!

This 9 mile line was in a sense a failure. It lost money, its slate traffic vanished when the Cambrian quarry succumbed to the slump and to attract business from the granite and limestone quarries, a spur had to be laid to an exchange siding on the G.W.R.

In 1888, with some revival in slate, the line was steamed and diverted to Chirk station with a slight increase of gauge to 2' 4½". The locomotives conformed to the then current street tramway practice of being boxed in and skirted almost to rail level, partly as a safety feature and partly to avoid frightening the horses! (Their more conventional 1917 Baldwin replacement was also unusual for a narrow gauge slate railway in being 4-6-0.)

At the same time the line was extended beyond Glyn Ceiriog to Hendre granite quarry to serve this and other stone quarries. Although the line was no longer canal owned, it did go beyond Chirk station to the canal at Chirk wharf. These new steam arrangements did not at first cater for passengers, but a full passenger and parcels service between Glyn and Chirk was put in in 1891.

The G.V.T. was an excellent example of a line, built for and supported by minerals revenues, serving a valuable social purpose as a passenger and general merchandise line promoting, as it did, a brick and tile works and two flannel factories, in what would otherwise have been an inaccessible valley.

The really notable development of the 1870's was the L. & N.W.R. Betws and Festiniog Railway which ran the 11½ miles from Betws-y-coed to Blaenau Ffestiniog and still forms the **Llandudno Junction-Blaenau Ffestiniog Branch**.

Commenced in 1872 at the height of the boom, it was not completed until 1879 in the depth of the slump. Thus although the blasting of a two mile tunnel through the unyielding rock of Moel Dyrnogydd was a triumph of Victorian enterprise, the decision to do so, as it turned out, was not.

Construction was started as a 2' gauge line, which had this been persisted with, would not only have been completed more quickly and cheaply but, connected to the F.R., could have readily siphoned off quarry traffic.

The first terminus was at Pantyrafon (SH697469) close to the Blaenau end of the tunnel where later a siding would run off to serve an exchange for Llechwedd quarry reached by a spur off their exit incline which ran down to the F.R. Dinas branch. In 1881 the Betws Extension took the line via some tricky bridging over the river Barlwyd to a new terminus immediately to the west of the town, which had exchange sidings linked to the F.R. Duffws branch. In 1873 the L. & N.W.R. had acquired Deganwy harbour on the Llandudno Junction-Llandudno branch, later adapting it for the transfer of 2' gauge wagons carried transversely in threes on transporter trucks.

In 1883 the Welsh Slate company put in an exchange at Pant yr Afon on the opposite side of the line from Llechwedd's, but the site was too cramped for efficient working and following the quarry's incorporation into Oakeley (itself an amalgamation of Holland's and Mathew's) little use was made of it.

Had this Conwy valley line reached Blaenau before the

F.R. was steamed, it might have captured a substantial slice of the Blaenau slate business, particularly as it could offer shipment at Deganwy free of harbour dues. As it was, with the Minffordd interchange in being and the slate industry in recession, it never fully justified the extensive ranks of interlocking narrow gauge – standard gauge exchange sidings at its Blaenau station. Its main immediate freight success was in general goods traffic which could be railed direct, instead of having to be re-handled at Minffordd, and domestic coal which could reach the coal merchants in colliery wagons.

Some traffic was picked up at Dolwyddelan, mainly from the Tyn y Bryn/Penllyn quarries (SH742521), this now combined unit becoming one of the very few slate quarries in Wales to have a standard gauge siding within its boundaries. Others carted to Dolwyddelan station, including Prince Llywelyn (SH744528) and Chwarel Fedw (SH748525), whose ¼ mile 2' gauge **Chwarel Fedw Tramway** was bridged by the railway without connection. Rhiw Goch quarry (SH749537) did plan an incline to the main road, with possible ideas of continuing it across the river to Pont y Pant station. The railway ran alongside both Pompren (SH726519) and Hendre (SH698512) quarries, but neither made connection. Their failure to do so emphasises the poor market conditions following the late 1870s slump. Nevertheless, it ended Dolwyddelan's isolation, and the hitherto remote fastnesses of the upper Lledr valley were served by Roman Bridge station.

The line had more success during the 1920s and 30s when it had considerable traffic in roadstone and when the decrepitude of the F.R. enabled it to increasingly capture Blaenau slate business.

Though not an immediate economic success, this railway was of immense social and commercial benefit to Blaenau, even more so than the steamed F.R. It enabled the town for the first time, to link itself with Conwy and the north coast and end its isolation from Bangor and Caernarfon. Besides which it shortened journey times to English cities, particularly Liverpool and the north. It also extended the labour catchment in a new direction. This was well illustrated when, during WW1 the Bwlch Gwyn quarry (SH767558) closed. Its adjacent settlement, the isolated, single-industry hamlet of Rhiwddolion, was able to survive as the men were able to find work in Blaenau quarries, by walking to Pont y Pant station.

A new F.R. station across the road from the L. & N.W.R. facilitated passenger interchange which encouraged journeys from Porthmadog to Conwy opening up yet another communications route.

It was post WW1, with the F.R. becoming progressively decrepit, that the L. & N.W.R. (now the L.M.S.R.) became of greater importance to Blaenau. The quarries increasingly used it to bring in coal for their dozens of boilers. When the Colloidal Slate Company was established, it was at Llandudno Junction, rather than Porthmadog which hitherto had been the natural location for Blaenau's downstream and support activities. This firm, an unusual co-operation between Oakeley and Llechwedd, was set up to coat Blaenau slates to meet the demand for coloured slates then being fostered by the Caernarfonshire, Cumberland and Pembrokeshire quarries. Although in 1930 Oakeley built an incline direct from their Glan y Don mill to the L.M.S.R. station and some well-publicised contracts were obtained, such as Coleg Harlech's warden's house, the venture was not a success and tonnages were trifling.

The L.M.S.R. had more success during the 1920s and 30s, handling granite roadstone chippings from Groby (SH696452) and Brookes (SH682437) quarries, each of which had branches to the F.R. These granite quarries being examples of other industry developing on the back of a slate-inspired railway.

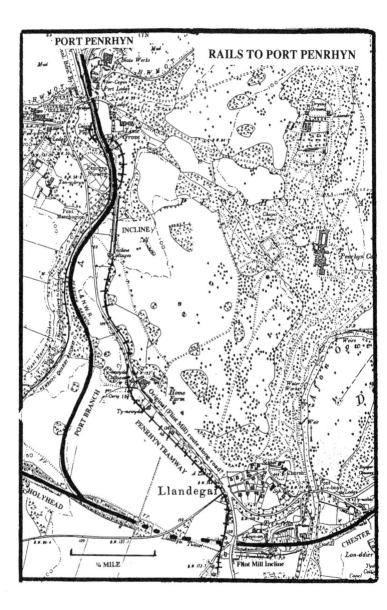

RAILS TO PORT PENRHYN

In south west Wales the relatively minuscule slate industry had little impact on railway building, and vice-versa. The association with slate of the 1856 broad gauge **South Wales Railway** (later Great Western) Gloucester to Neyland (then New Milford), was trifling. Had it run to its initial objective Fishguard, rather than New Milford, it might have benefited the north Pembrokeshire quarries and if a feeder line from the eastern Cleddau valley had been built, its unique variety of slate might have found wider acceptance. All this was symptomatic of the S.W.R.'s 'through Wales not to Wales' attitude, illustrated by the fact that although it ran through Carmarthen, St. Clears and Haverfordwest, then ports of considerable local importance, it had no quayside connections at any of them.

It was partly the failure of the S.W.R. to reach Fishguard that gave rise to the broad gauge **Carmarthen and Cardigan Railway**, planned to provide the by then G.W.R. with a seaport terminal on the Teifi estuary near Cemaes Head. Planned in 1854 it adopted the Great North & South Wales route leaving the S.W.R. at Johnston west of Carmarthen, smashing its way straight through the town, swinging through Newcastle Emlyn and, via various tunnels, arriving at Cilgerran, where it was to demolish the back gardens of every property on the north side of the main street! Whilst this plan was not primarily a slate railway, Nant yr Hebog quarry (SN418328) did appear on the plans and the extraordinary route through Cilgerran must surely have been chosen to serve the Teifi gorge workings. Included were feeder branches to tap the collieries of eastern Carmarthenshire.

As eventually built, the total devastation of Carmarthen was avoided by running east from Carmarthen station, and reducing its tunnel requirements to one by snaking through valleys. The line opened in 1864, without the colliery feeders and no nearer Cardigan than Llandysul. Although extended to Newcastle Emlyn in 1895 (by this time standard gauge of course), it never did reach Cardigan but it did raise interest in some small slate workings on its route. At Pengraigygigfran (SN420326), a siding was made to connect with a tramway from the quarry but outputs from here and the other diggings proved insignificant. The line was third-railed from Pencader Junction to Carmarthen in 1867 forming part of the spectacularly misnamed Manchester & Milford Railway coming in from Aberystwyth. This opened up south Wales markets to the Aberystwyth slate finishing factories which flourished towards the end of the century.

Slate certainly played no part in the strategy of the **Central Wales Railway** (L. & N.W.R.). However, the reverse did occur in that it created a flurry of activity, investment and local employment at several tiny diggings near Llanwrtyd Wells, following its 1868 completion.

Similarly it was probably the anticipation of the 1865 opening of the Llanelli Railway's **Llandilo-Carmarthen** line which encouraged the development of Pantyglien quarry (SN465224) in 1864 and may possibly have spurred the concurrent development of Llwynypiod quarry (SN433229).

In balance the effect of railways on south west Wales slate was definitely negative, since they made it easier and cheaper to bring in better slate from north Wales. This was exemplified in 1880 when Maenclochog mill, which stands within sight of Rosebush quarry (SN079300), was re-roofed, the quarry's own railway was used to bring in north Wales slate!

Nevertheless there were two entirely slate-inspired standard gauge lines both of which appreciably and generally beneficial to the areas they served. The first was the **Whitland and Taf Vale Railway** of 1873. Beginning at Whitland it ran west for 2¼ miles along a third-railed section of the G.W.R. main line before diverging north-west. Although it would eventually reach Cardigan, its primary objective was Glogue slate quarry (SN320328) whose proprietor was the line's main sponsor. A siding gave

Glogue direct access and two other quarries had tramway connection. In addition Llanglywen station offered a loading facility for slate carted from the eastern Cleddau quarries. Terminating at Crymych, the line helped agriculture in what had hitherto been a marginalised area. It also catered for several lead workings, but in doing so hastened the decline of the port of St Clears.

The other line was the 8¼ mile **Maenclochog Railway**, the only Standard Gauge railway in Wales to be built and owned by a slate company. It ran from a junction on the G.W.R. at Narberth Road (later Clynderwen) to Rosebush quarry (SN073300). Planned in 1869 at the height of the slate boom, it opened in 1876 barely a year before the slate market collapsed. Apart from this unfortunate timing, a full scale railway for a small and marginal quarry was overambitious since even its peak output would have scarcely filled one train a week. Efforts to promote its tourist potential were unsuccessful, but it did bring undoubted benefits to the southern Preseli area. Benefits which were widened when, as the north Pembrokeshire Railway, it was extended to Fishguard in 1895. The N.P.R.'s role as a Fishguard connection was usurped by the G.W.R. line from Clarbeston Road in 1906, but it continued to serve a sparsely populated area which without the original slate sponsored line would not have had a rail service.

Also outside the mainstream slate areas was the **Llanfflewyn Tramway** which sought to carry the output of the eponymous Anglesey quarry at SH347892, some ½ mile across Llyn Llygeirian. Built c.1874 it failed to survive the late 1870s slump.

9. The 1870s. Narrow Gauge Steam

The North Wales Narrow Gauge, Penrhyn, Corris & Gorseddau

During the 1870s four new narrow gauge steam lines were opened. The most spectacular for both the grandeur of its concept and the scale of its economic failure, was the **North Wales Narrow Gauge Railway**.

This 1' 11½" line arose out of several local initiatives to bring rails to the parts of north west Wales which had proved economically unattractive to the main line companies.

The original N.W.N.G.R. general undertaking was an odd rag bag of routes. One route was to make an end-on junction at Beddgelert with the proposed Croesor & Port Madoc Extension Railway. This branch of the Croesor & Port Madoc Railway, which had taken on ownership of the lower part of the Croesor tramway in 1865, was to run from the Croesor at Garreg Hylldrem along the east bank of the Glaslyn to terminate opposite Beddgelert church. On the assumption that this branch would be built and the Croesor relaid in heavier track, the N.W.N.G.R. would lay their new line from it, along Nant Gwynant, reaching Pen y Gwryd via switch-backs, and on to Betws-y-coed where it would reach the L. & N.W.R. Continuing eastward along the present A5, there would be a branch along the Machno valley to Cwm Machno and at Cerrigydrudion it would meet the proposed Ruthin and Cerrigydrudion Railway and terminate at Corwen station on the G.W.R. Ruabon-Dolgellau branch.

A separate line was to run from Caernarfon and via the Gwyrfai valley reach Rhyd Ddu, the planned terminus of a railway to Snowdon summit. There would be a branch to Moel Tryfan, whose slate traffic together with that from Cwm Gwyrfai, Nant Gwynant, Dyffryn Llugwy and Cwm

Machno, would support a full rail service for places such as Beddgelert, Capel Curig, Pentrefoelas and Cerrigydrudion.

The whole deal was also to include a line to Porth Dinllaen from Pwllheli, which would be reached from Porthmadog by either new track or by third-railing the Cambrian. This fixation with Porth Dinllaen is curious since although rails there would have been of local benefit, developing it as a port was by now a dead duck. Actually the N.W.N.G.R. were not the last to have such ideas. In 1877 immediately it became apparent that the N.W.N.G.R. were not going to build to Porth Dinllaen, the Cambrian Railways sought to revive their earlier plans to extend from Pwllheli and after this lapsed it was revived yet again in 1884 as the Porth Dinllaen Railway. As late as 1913 the Cambrian were still planning to reach there.

The N.W.N.G.R. failed to get approval for most of its routes, leaving it with just the Beddgelert to Betws-y-coed section and the Rhyd Ddu line with its Moel Tryfan branch. This latter's access to Caernarfon was blocked by objections from the L. & N.W.R. so was forced to commence at an interchange at Dinas on the Caernarfon-Afon Wen branch some three miles south of Caernarfon.

Unsurprisingly in view of the engineering difficulties of reaching Capel Curig from Nant Gwynant, and with the Beddgelert-Porthmadog link in doubt, the Betws line was never attempted. This left them with just one line which effectively ran from a small village to a bare hilltop, but did of course assist the development of quarries on Moel Tryfan and in Cwm Gwyrfai, filling a gap left by the non-building of the sub-branches of the L. & N.W.R. Llanberis branch.

The scheme had been given impetus by the success of the steamed Ffestiniog and the Talyllyn railways, but unlike the F.R. it did not reach a port and unlike the Talyllyn it ran to a railway by necessity rather than choice. It also broke new ground in being the first Welsh narrow gauge line to use 6-

coupled locos, and the only one to exclusively use them. The original Vulcan foundry pair were 0-6-4- single Fairlies, their subsequent two Hunslets had the same wheel layout (one Fairlie, one rigid). Even Russell which they 'inherited' in 1906, was a 2-6-2.

The transfer of slate into standard gauge wagons at Dinas was a relatively costly operation, with breakages abounding. Plus, although the slate was meant to reach Caernarfon quays, like loadings of Nantlle material at Talysarn, once aboard L. & N.W.R. wagons, it tended to stay there, thus hastening Caernarfon's demise as a port.

Like the L. & N.W.R.'s Blaenau line, the N.W.N.G.R. had been planned in the heady days of the early 1870s, and like the L. & N.W.R. its opening coincided with the collapse of the slate market. Besides which, although the quality of rock on Moel Tryfan was good, that in Cwm Gwyrfai proved disappointing, in addition the population catchment was minimal.

Partly opening in 1877, it reached the full 11 miles to its eventual terminus at Rhyd Ddu in 1881 (having sold and leased back all their locos to pay for it!). Rhyd Ddu was a desolate spot with two small and two minuscule quarries as possible freight customers and a few knickerbockered, Snowdon-bound climbers as potential passengers who would wait in vain for a railway to Snowdon summit.

From Rhyd Ddu the line ran down the Gwyrfai valley for some 6 miles to Waunfawr, passing about ten slate quarries, only four of which ever had connections and only one of these, Glanrafon (SH581540), was ever able to contribute worthwhile tonnages. From Waunfawr it turned west for a further 5 miles to reach Dinas. In spite of following a relatively easy route, quite extensive civil work was involved, particularly near its upper end where it had to contour-chase the valley flank, crossing a number of streams and rivers, as well as going under half a dozen roads.

There were intermediate passenger/goods stations at

Cwellyn, Plas y Nant, Salem, Betws Garmon, Waunfawr and Tryfan Junction. At Tryfan Junction the Bryngwyn branch which supplied most of the freight, joined. The original plan had called for a branch which would make a sinuous climb up from a junction about 4 miles from Dinas. Instead Tryfan Junction was sited just over 2 miles from Dinas with height being gained from there by loops, stiff climbs of circa 1 in 30 and finally a half-mile long, self-acting balanced incline which raised the line 350' to almost 900'. This branch ran to the area which the Carnarvon & Llandwrog Railway had aimed to serve and enabled a group of reasonably productive quarries on Moel Tryfan to survive during a time of slump, and to bring in the coal on which they were substantially dependent.

Besides being the most heavily used, this branch was also the most interesting part of the line. At the head of the incline, it split into four sub-branches. One snaked north for 1½ miles, rising a further 350' to the largest quarry, Alexandra (SH519562). A second was a short section which met the long incline down from Moel Tryfan quarry (SH515559). The third ran south east for about ¼ mile to meet via a switchback, a new incline down from Braich quarry (SH510552).

The fourth left this Braich line to make its leisurely way through Fron village to Fron quarry (SH515548) also picking up business from some small, unconnected quarries. This Braich/Fron layout which opened in 1881 replaced the 3' 6" John Robinson line which had connected Braich and Fron with the Nantlle Railway via Talysarn quarry (SH496534). In 1895 Pen yr Orsedd quarry (SH510538) considered using the N.W.N.G.R. instead of the Nantlle, but this was not done presumably because of the uphaulage which would have been needed. This idea was revived in 1922 by Cilgwyn. Doubtless stirred by the reincarnation of the N.W.N.G.R. as the Welsh Highland Railway, they deserted the Nantlle

Railway and joined the Fron branch via a short link from their 'horseshoe' tipping line.

This line illustrates the shortage of tipping space which bedevilled Nantlle slate operations. A number of small quarries were bought up by larger neighbours purely as dumps. Cilgwyn boldly attacked the problem by establishing a tip at SH500549 which was reached by this steeply climbing steam line. The embankment of the line absorbed around a quarter of a million tons of waste rock apart from what went onto the tip itself, every ton of which had to be expensively shunted up a stiff gradient.

To Cilgwyn, dispatching output by a spanking new steam railway rather than by antiquated horse wagons must have seemed an excellent idea at the time, but in the end the Nantlle would prove more reliable and outlast the N.W.N.G.R./W.H.R. by a quarter of a century.

The N.W.N.G.R.'s safety record was not outstanding, passenger train derailments (happily usually without casualties) were not a rarity and mechanical failures were routine. In spite of this, its running battle with the Railway Inspectors and constant financial problems, exacerbated by the financial shakiness of many of its quarry customers, at its turn of the century peak the N.W.N.G.R. was carrying over 25,000 tons of slate per annum, a respectable 5% of the total Welsh output.

The main line also carried stone and iron ore and was of appreciable economic benefit to Betws Garmon, Waunfawr and the Gwyrfai valley generally. The Bryngwyn branch was a lifeline to quarrying settlements such as Rhostryfan, where there was a station, and Rhosgadfan and Y Fron which were not too far from the passenger terminus at Bryngwyn at the foot of the incline.

The line's value to the community as a whole was demonstrated by its over 50,000 passengers and around 700 tons of coal and general goods carried each year during the late 1890s.

In the meantime at Penrhyn the horse tramway which had been giving sterling service since the beginning of the century was by now somewhat anachronistic. Dinorwig, their main competitor had been hauling their output to port by steam locomotives for thirty years, and had also been introducing them at quarry and port since the beginning of the decade. It was certainly extraordinary that with the 20th century approaching, the largest and probably most profitable quarry in the world was still relying on a line designed in the 18th century. Now carrying throughputs several times those envisaged almost 80 years earlier, it was only by running trains of up to 50 or more wagons and suffering serious delays at the inclines, that the daily movement of 250-300 tons could be dealt with.

Since around 1870 there had been substantial alterations in the quarry inclines down to Coed y Parc and by the mid 70s much of the route near the upper end had been upgraded. In spite of blandishments from C.E. Spooner, to allow him to emulate his successful steam conversion of the Ffestiniog and continue the upgraded line to the port, the elderly proprietor, Edward Gordon Douglas-Pennant recently ennobled as Lord Penrhyn, seems to have shown an entrenched resistance to change, which was causing his quarry to stagnate and be overtaken by Dinorwig.

At the same time he was beset by a clamour to permit a standard gauge branch to be run to Bethesda. This he staunchly opposed because of its potential advantage to the several small quarries, which to his chagrin operated just outside of his boundaries and because it would have eroded his position as a monopoly employer.

Since Lord Penrhyn carried enough clout to block any Act, the L. & N.W.R. sought to appease him by offering to build a narrow gauge branch between their proposed Bethesda station and Coed y Parc thus enabling Penrhyn quarry to enjoy the speed and efficiency which they claimed their railway would be able to offer. Stung by such an arrogant implication of inadequacy of his own line, and the realisation that he would have to modernise to stay in the game, Lord Penrhyn immediately set about introducing steam traction on the railway, in the quarry and at the port.

It perhaps should be mentioned that this Lord Penrhyn was, properly, Baron Penrhyn of Llandygái. This title had no connection with that of his kinsman the 'Old' Lord Penrhyn, whose title, Baron Penrhyn of Penrhyn, County Louth had been extinguished on his death in 1808.

Just as construction of the existing line had been pressed forward by this previous Lord Penrhyn in a time of bad trade, so fortuitously did the building of the new **Penrhyn Railway** (completed in 1879), coincide with the slump. Thus not only minimising the problems of the interruptions which the construction caused, but also the economies the new line brought helped the quarry through the difficulties of the 1880s.

At 1' 11" it was effectively the same gauge as the old line and a more circuitous route obviated the need for inclines. Thus it avoided the transporter trucks and crewling down to port which were now proving a handicap to Dinorwig.

The route, which with hindsight seems so obvious was not immediately chosen, although the first idea closely followed the eventual route as far as the head of the Dinas incline. From there instead of dropping in to the Cegin valley, it would have reached the port by third railing the standard gauge port branch. Public service would be provided by a line from Coed y Parc to Bethesda (thus in effect reversing the L. & N.W.R. proposal), and by a branch from near Tregarth to a new station alongside Bangor main line station.

An amended plan took a more direct route through a tunnel north of Bangor. A further idea was to join the main line immediately east of its existing Bangor tunnel and third railing it to Bangor station. This latter scheme included a very odd branch to Pentir possibly due to the alleged slate potential on Moel Rhiwen south of Rhiwlas.

The advantages to Lord Penrhyn of these layouts would have been twofold. They would have effectively scotched the L. & N.W.R.'s Bethesda branch ambitions. They would also put a stop to the long-standing visions of a narrow gauge line which, running over non-Penrhyn land, would connect the independent quarries to a new port east of Bangor, but which could not have been viable without general traffic.

The line as built ran from Coed y Parc roughly paralleling its predecessor as far as the head of the Cilgeraint incline. From there it took a wide sweep around Tregarth to the head of the Dinas incline. From here the new route dived down into the Cegin valley, following its eastern bank to just short of Port Penrhyn. A loop in the river barred the approach to the port, but since the standard gauge port branch was quarry owned, the crossing and re-crossing was made by widening the standard gauge bridges.

Most of the quarry and port locomotives were by now mostly vertical boilered De Wintons. Although a Falcon loco and anecdotally one by Hughes, Valley Foundry Anglesey were initially used on the railway, the basic engines were three conventional horizontal-boilered De Wintons. These were later replaced by more powerful Hunslets. All were the usual 0-4-0's. Since there were worries about side clearance along the line, the De Wintons most exceptionally had inside cylinders while the Hunslets had compacted valve gear with raised cylinders.

No provision was made for the public carriage of passengers or goods. Workmen travelling daily were carried in rudimentary carriages (which at first were totally open), but the weekly barrackers such as the Anglesey men coming over by ferry to Port Penrhyn each Monday morning, were, initially at least, carried in ordinary wagons. Restricting travel to employees prevented Bethesda men from using it to seek work outside the village and at the same time widening Penrhyn's labour catchment area.

Although the workmen's trains only ran to suit the quarry start and finish times and there was never any authorisation as a public railway, unofficial use on a 'family and friends' basis, may have been quite extensive.

Returning to the south of Gwynedd, slate traffic on the Corris, Machynlleth & River Dovey Tramroad, had failed to meet expectations. An initial idea of extending the Upper Corris Tramway to the Tir Stint ironstone mine at SH760164 had been trotted out again in 1863. This 6 mile line would have climbed by a stiff 1 in 24 gradient, winding to cross and re-cross the main road. It would have curved around Mynydd Dol Ffanog, passed through a 75 yard tunnel, crossed the road near the summit of Bwlch Llyn Bach and dived down in grades up to 1 in 46 to Tir Stint. It was of course never built and neither was the other extension to Glyn Iago slate quarry (SH719072), which could have also catered for quarries such as Ty'n y Ceunant (SH744088). Formations and an incline for the latter were built in the late 1890s but never completed.

Also in 1863, less than four years after the C.M. & R.D. tramway had opened, there had been a scheme to supersede it altogether with a standard gauge steam railway. Although innocuously calling itself an extension to the C.M. & R.D., it in fact entirely ignored its existence. Leaving the Aberystwyth & Welch Coast just east of Machynlleth, it would have closely followed the Afon Dulas, crossing and re-crossing it as well as diverting it with careless arrogance. Still keeping close to the river, it would have run past Aberllefenni, struck due north up the Ceiswyn valley to Ratgoed. Maintaining a 1 in 25 climb it would have tunnelled for 1938 yards under Mynydd Ceiswyn emerging to cross the Talyllyn-Cross Foxes road and run down to Tir Stint. It would have continued on, crossing the Cross Foxes-Dolgellau road at SH757182, dropping down in a 1 in 35

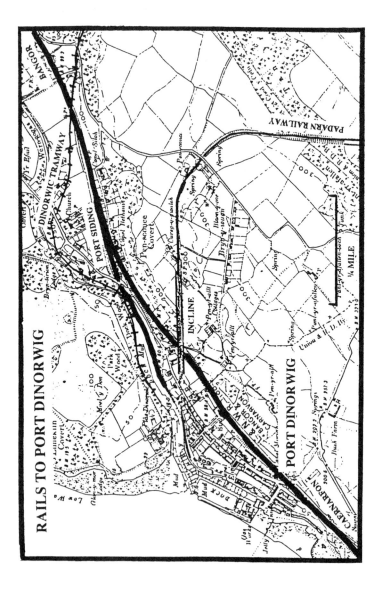

RAILS TO PORT DINORWIG

PORT DINORWIG

grade past Brithdir, to curve around to join the then projected Bala-Dolgellau line.

Unextended and unmodernised the C.M. & R.D. soldiered on until 1879, when it was relaid, steamed and renamed the **Corris Railway**. The timing was unfortunate since like the N.W.N.G.R. and others, it almost exactly coincided with the slump, which hit the Corris producers particularly hard. Consequently the upgrading of the line failed to generate the anticipated increase in slate traffic, particularly as the charges which its light traffic density forced it to impose, eroded the competitiveness of its quarry customers. (At this time the Corris Railway was handling less than 10,000 tons p.a. whereas the Penrhyn, Padarn and Ffestiniog were each handling around ten times as much.) To add to the C.R.'s difficulties, as a result of the bad trade, quarry customers were failing to settle their accounts. Theoretically the C.R. could refuse to carry any further shipments, but in practice this would have closed the quarry, losing them business and landing them with a bad debt.

There had probably been some passenger carrying since the early 1870s and although there was an official passenger service just prior to steaming, regular steam passenger trains did not commence until 1883, with mixed running of horse-drawn coaches and steam hauled trucks in the interim. Population catchment was larger than say, the Talyllyn, and apart from the termini and Corris stations, there were halts at Garneddwen, Pont Ifans, Escairgeiliog, Llwyngwern, Lliwdy, Doldderwen and Ffridd Gate, so that there were ample opportunities for passengers to use it. However its passenger potential fell far short of the F.R.'s so the contribution passenger revenue could make towards overheads was limited.

However it did put Aberllefenni and Corris squarely on the railway map, and helped to ensure their survival as viable communities even after the near obliteration of quarrying at Corris in 1906. None of this was good news for

Aberdyfi for inexorably an increasing proportion of the reduced tonnages transferred to the Cambrian Railways at Machynlleth remained on rail instead of being dropped off at the port.

The three original Falcon locomotives were saddle tanks with the usual 0-4-0 wheel arrangement although they were later rebuilt to 0-4-2, this layout being specified for their later Kerr Stuart engine.

The fourth narrow gauge line of the 1870s, though grand in concept proved to be of trifling importance and on the strength of briefly using one De Winton locomotive, this revival of the Gorseddau line just qualified as a steam railway. (Although commonplace within quarries, this is the only known instance of a vertical boilered De Winton being used cross country.)

The pressure to exploit undeveloped slate occurrences had continued in areas such as Cwm Pennant. In 1861 before the awesome scale of the Gorseddau debacle had become apparent, new owners at nearby Hendre Ddu quarry (SH519444) had obtained wayleaves to run a railway down the western side of the valley to Cricieth. Besides serving Hendre Ddu, it could have offered rail connection to several promising slate sites in Dolbenmaen such as Tyddyn Mawr (SH506428). With a possible northerly extension to other slate quarries and copper mines, the line could have made Cricieth a slate and minerals port and an exchange point with the Cambrian Railways.

One of the quarries this line might have served was the Prince of Wales (SH549498) a small working still carrying by packhorse over to the Gwyrfai valley for cartage to Caernarfon. In 1872, the year when Hendre Ddu's failure put an end to the Cricieth scheme, extensive and expensive redevelopment of the Prince of Wales quarry was begun. Rather than take on the Cricieth proposal, the presumably cheaper option of buying the now defunct Gorseddau line was chosen, relaying it in 2' gauge and extending for 4 miles from Braich y Bib (SH552441), under the extravagant title, the **Gorseddau Junction and Portmadoc Railways**.

Opened in 1875, the extension did not match the high standard of the original formations. Arrangements at the Porthmadog end were simplified by abandoning the last few hundred yards of the original route, making a junction with the Croesor and running on its metals to the wharves.

The quarry being scarcely more successful than its Gorseddau predecessor, the solitary locomotive found little employment. An extension to Cwm Dwyfor copper mine at the head of the valley brought little additional trade and it was not practicable for the quarries on the western side of the valley to use it, although immediately the line opened, Dolgarth slate quarry (SH538495) was advertised for sale as being '600 yards from the Gorseddau Junction Railway, to which it could be joined'. The difference in levels would have made this difficult.

Unlike the original Gorseddau, this revived line had the possibility of connecting with the standard gauge at Porthmadog, and had a passenger service been run, there would have been a spur to the north side of the Cambrian station. A full slate exchange facility on the Beddgelert siding, opposite to Croesor depot was planned, but since traffic proved to be almost as sparse as it had been in the line's previous incarnation, this ended up as just a spur into the Cambrian cattle yard.

By 1878 horses had replaced the loco and by 1890 solitary trucks were being hand pushed to Porthmadog.

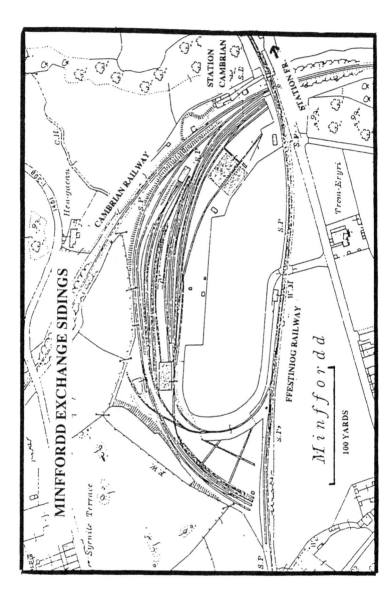

MINFFORDD EXCHANGE SIDINGS

CAMBRIAN RAILWAY

STATION
CAMBRIAN

FFESTINIOG RAILWAY

Minffordd

100 YARDS

10. 1880s and on. The Final Bids

In the rip-roaring days of the early 1870s, Holland and other Blaenau slate proprietors, dissatisfied with the Ffestiniog Railway and with the poor access it then offered to the Cambrian Railways at Porthmadog, had proposed a new and independent route for their products based on extending the Festiniog & Blaenau Railway.

The scheme, the Merionethshire Railway (which confusingly had been an early name for the Bala-Dolgellau line), called for converting the Festiniog & Blaenau Railway to mixed gauge and extending it to near the present Trawsfynydd power station. From there it would turn west to run along what is now the lake bed, parallel to and to the south of the present private road to the reservoir dam. After crossing the Afon Prysor, it would then have swung north west to dive down alongside the Prysor gorge and just short of the Maentwrog-Harlech road would have turned west to a triangular junction with the Cambrian (nee Aberdovey & Welch Coast) line just north of Llandecwyn station. By some judicious curves and a 172 yard tunnel near the lower end, the 10 mile line would keep its maximum grade to 1 in 40 although some curves would be as tight as 6 chains radius.

The depth of anti-F.R., feeling at the time is shown by the suggestion that a line should also be laid linking the Holland and Llechwedd quarries with the F. & B. terminus at Blaenau, enabling those quarries to access the new Merionethshire connection without passing over F.R. metals.

Apart from the problems of reaching the Cambrian having been eased by the Minffordd interchange, the Merionethshire scheme was overtaken by the Bala & Ffestiniog railway proposal. In this Holland joined with Henry Robertson in what was in essence a revival of the unbuilt part of Robertson's 1860s Corwen, Bala & Portmadoc Railway. Having been beaten to Porthmadog by the Cambrian and now threatened to be bested by the L. &

N.W.R.'s Conwy valley line, the G.W.R. enthusiastically backed the plans.

By the late 1870s with the arrival of the L. & N.W.R. at Blaenau imminent and the slate trade diving into deep recession, there was little reason for the Bala to Ffestiniog link, but impelled by the G.W.R.'s determination to penetrate north of the Mawddach, it seems to have taken on a dogged dynamism of its own, resulting in the building of what would become the 25½ mile **Bala-Blaenau Branch**, operated by the G.W.R. and fully incorporated in 1910. It was one of the most expensive (over 70 bridges and viaducts plus miles of cuttings, embankments and ledges), and probably the least profitable of all Welsh railways.

In spite of vociferous objections from the Merionethshire sponsors (including Holland!), that it would take traffic from their still unbuilt line, part opened in 1882, it reached Blaenau in 1884. It ran from a junction near Bala station on the Ruabon-Dolgellau line to Bala town and up the Derwen valley to near the head of Cwm Prysor which it crossed by a fine viaduct. From there to Trawsfynydd, it clung precariously to the side of the valley, offering grand views to the few passengers that used it. From the vicinity of the present power station, it approximately followed the route surveyed for the Merionethshire line to Llan Ffestiniog. It bought out and relaid the Festiniog & Blaenau Railway and F.R. platform at their Blaenau station offered an easy interchange, which eventually became the F.R.'s passenger terminus, leaving Duffws to solely handle freight.

Although this line effectively extinguished all reason for the Merionethshire project, it did not extinguish a determination to build it. In 1884, the Merionethshire company proposed running just from Llandecwyn to Trawsfynydd, where there would be a large triangular junction with the G.W.R. Fortunately for the sponsors' pockets, this idea was soon abandoned.

The Bala-Blaenau branch's sole 'new' slate business was

picked up at Maentwrog Road station from the small Braich Ddu slate quarry (SH718384), whose transport problems had been considerable since boating on the Dwyryd had ceased in 1868. This quarry taking the opportunity to stage one of its frequent brief revivals, planned to build a tramway to the new branch, but only a few hundred yards at the quarry end were completed.

All other slate traffic was inherited from the F. & B., a little from the workings around Llan Ffestiniog but most from Graig Ddu, its slate wagons being loaded at Tan y Manod (site of the original F. & B. Manod station) onto transporter trucks to be taken to Blaenau station. Some slate was transferred there into standard gauge trucks to go back down to Bala Junction but most found its way onto the F.R. via the same narrow gauge link which had served the F. & B. Some may have even made its way across the town to the L. & N.W.R.! It was of course theoretically possible for any Blaenau quarry to reach the G.W.R. by working across on F.R. metals, but few if any did so.

To encourage the quarries to use its railway the G.W.R. provided 2' gauge slate wagons for their convenience. These wagons being built to the usual G.W.R. standards were highly prized bits of kit and were frequently seen in various quarries and on the F.R.! (The corresponding L. & N.W.R. wagons were equally good but they never quite achieved the cult status of the G.W.R. items.)

In all the Bala branch was even less successful in robbing the F.R. than had been the L. & N.W.R. With that line already established it did not even serve to force down the F.R.'s rates. Like the L. & N.W.R., it developed, during the early 20th century, a useful trade in roadstone from Arenig quarry (SH830392) and a little from Pengwern (SH707450) and Madog (SH708448) quarries (laying a spur to the latter), but as a slate carrier it mainly took over the F. & B.'s role as a feeder to the F.R.

This Bala to Blaenau line of course improved on the F. & B.'s

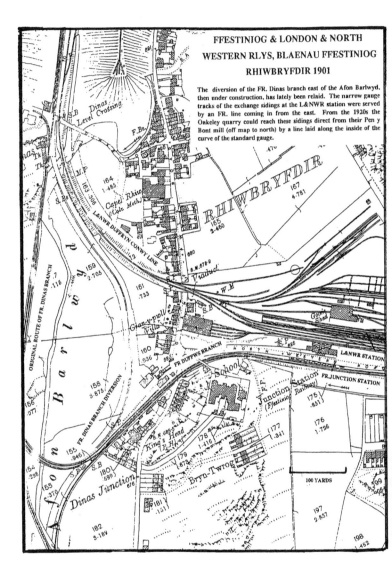

FFESTINIOG & LONDON & NORTH
WESTERN RLYS, BLAENAU FFESTINIOG
RHIWBRYFDIR 1901

The diversion of the FR. Dinas branch east of the Afon Barlwyd,
then under construction, has lately been relaid. The narrow gauge
tracks of the exchange sidings at the L&NWR station were served
by an FR. line coming in from the east. From the 1920s the
Oakeley quarry could reach these sidings direct from their Pen y
Bont mill (off map to north) by a line laid along the inside of the
curve of the standard gauge.

144

passenger and goods service and extended them to Trawsfynydd and the small communities of the Prysor and Tryweryn valleys. It is an exaggeration to say that it stopped at every farm but in spite of much of its route being in thinly populated country, it did have 16 intermediate stations and halts.

Blaenau being already well served by the L. & N.W.R. Conwy valley branch, the G.W.R.'s economic effect was not dramatic, but had some potential to widen the Blaenau quarries' area of labour catchment. Possibly the line's greatest impact was its enabling a large military training camp to be sited at Bronaber from the 1900s to the 1950s, for which there was a special station at Trawsfynydd.

However the line did serve a most important if less tangible social, cultural and political function in uniting Blaenau Ffestiniog the economic powerhouse of Meirionnydd with its religious and linguistic heartland at Bala, as well as easing communications with the county town of Dolgellau and putting Blaenau in more ready touch with industrial north east Wales. This social benefit might have been widened had it been possible to make a junction with the L. & N.W.R. at Blaenau enabling through working between Conwy and Bala. With the F.R. controlling the intervening land, this was not an option, but the interchange between the F.R. and the G.W.R. being merely a platform's width, enabled travellers from Porthmadog to Bala to circumvent a bleak wait at Barmouth Junction. Additionally, the erstwhile Bala station having been closed, a shuttle service between Bala Junction and the new Bala station meant that arrivals from Dolgellau or Corwen were spared almost three-quarters of a rainswept mile to reach the town.

The line was notable for carrying one commodity, quite out of keeping with Bala's Calvinistic Methodist connections – Welsh whisky from 'Squire' Lloyd Price's Fron Goch distillery!

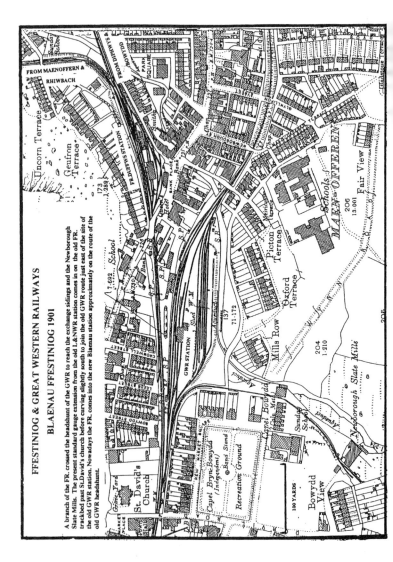

FFESTINIOG & GREAT WESTERN RAILWAYS
BLAENAU FFESTINIOG 1901

A branch of the FR. crossed the headshunt of the GWR to reach the exchange sidings and the Newborough Slate Mills. The present standard gauge extension from the old L&NWR station comes in on the old FR. trackbed past St.David's church before curving slightly south to join the old GWR route just east of the site of the old GWR station. Nowadays the FR. comes into the new Blaenau station approximately on the route of the old GWR headshunt.

FROM MAENOFFERN & RHIWBACH

Uncorn Terrace

Genfron Terrace

173 1.289

FROM DINWYS

FROM DINWYS STATION

PARK SQUARE

BOWYDD

CROWELL STREET

BOWYDD STREET

7.692

School

School

S.P.

S.P.

S.P.

S.P.

Aqueduct

Shed W.M

GWR STATION

71.172

139

MAEN-OFFEREN

Schools

Fair View

206 13.001

Picton Terrace

Oxford Terrace

Mills Row

204 1.210

Newborough Slate Mills

St. David's Church

Grave Yard

MARKET PLACE

Capel Bryn-Bowydd (Independent)

Bend Stand

Recreation Ground

Capel Bowydd

Sunday School

Bowydd View

Fair View

100 YARDS

By the early 1880s George Douglas-Pennant (who in 1886 would become the notorious second Baron), was becoming increasingly critical of what he perceived to be his octogenarian father's lax handling of the Penrhyn quarry's affairs. It is difficult to imagine that George would favour anything which diluted the quarry's labour monopoly or benefited the other Bethesda workings. In fact his attitude towards competitors would be shown in 1885 when he did at last wrest control from his father's failing grasp, and he cut off the water supply to the totally water-powered Bryn Hafod y Wern quarry (SH631693). It may be that the old man wished to demonstrate that he was still the boss, but for whatever reason he acceded to the L. & N.W.R.'s wish to build a railway to Bethesda and in 1884 the 4½ mile **Bethesda Branch** was opened, the very last slate-inspired standard gauge railway in north west Wales.

It left the main line immediately east of the Bangor tunnel, crossed the Cegin valley by a seven arch viaduct, before turning east to reach the Ogwen valley by the 297 yard Tregarth tunnel and bridging the river by a five arch structure, to run to Bethesda along its east bank.

It was a counterpart of the Llanberis branch, but it failed to have the same re-vitalising effect on the independent quarries of Bethesda, as had the Llanberis line on those to the south-west of Llyn Padarn. This was because the potential of the independents in the Ogwen valley was limited, the times did not favour development and none ever had direct connection.

As a general carrier the branch was of service to the town but quarry supplies obviously continued to come in on the Penrhyn Railway, as indeed did commuting quarrymen. Bethesda failed to develop a Llanberis-type tourist trade and the two intermediate stations, Felin Hen and Tregarth both served very small communities, yet passenger numbers as a percentage of catchment population was possibly the highest for any comparable railway in Wales which is indicative of its importance to the Bethesda and the Ogwen valley. Having a tunnel, cuttings, embankments, and seven viaducts and bridges, its per-mile cost must have exceeded even the Bala-Ffestiniog Railway, and its construction would never have been undertaken without the possibility of slate traffic.

Although this railway failed to carry much slate it was indirectly of considerable importance to the industry and to the slate communities. It is arguable that this railway enabled W.J. Parry, the moving spirit behind the North Wales Quarrymen's Union, to rise from being a village ironmonger to become a substantial merchant, which considerably increased his influence, especially during the 1900-1903 stoppage. Parry was able to ameliorate the hardships of the stoppage by setting up a co-operative to work Tan y Bwlch (SH628683) and Pantdreiniog (SH623671) quarries. Since both were heavy coal users, they could not have survived without the rail-supplied coal yard at Bethesda.

In fact the survival of Bethesda itself would have been in jeopardy without this non-Penrhyn controlled link. Plus it facilitated access by journalists such as Clement Edwards, who made the Penrhyn dispute a national issue and a turning point in industrial relations.

At about the same time as the Bala-Blaenau and the Bethesda branches were being planned, there had been another proposal which might have resulted in a railway which would have carried no goods or passengers, yet would have been extremely influential, the Nantlle Vale Drainage & Tramway Bill of 1880.

With the whole of the floor of the Nantlle valley being almost solid slate, quarry waste had to be dumped on to good rock while pumping became increasingly onerous as the workings deepened. This imaginative dual scheme would have provided unified pumped drainage for all the major quarries and a tramway due west to enable all waste to be tipped into the sea. If local squabbling had not killed off this plan, the Nantlle quarries would not have come to an early halt choked to death on their own rubbish.

In 1884, there was in south Wales, near Carmarthen, another 'rubbish railway' proposal which though trifling, might have been a portent of greater things. The Patent Slate Brick and Sanitary Tube Company proposed the Llwynpiod Tramway, which would have been a ¾ mile, horse-drawn roadside line linking Llwynpiod quarry (SN433229) with Dolgwili brickworks (SN430218). The intention being to enable the brickworks to utilise the quarry tips as raw material. Although a number of quarries utilised waste to produce by-products such as powders, bricks, etc., to have had a rail link to an independent, off site specialist firm would have been unique and might well have set an important precedent.

In the same area, the Carmarthen and Cardigan Railway having as it were, run out of steam at Newcastle Emlyn, had long abandoned any hope of attaining its eponymous goal. In the meantime, the Whitland & Taf Vale line, having renamed itself the **Whitland and Cardigan Railway**, crept on towards Cardigan, reaching there in 1885. Its just over 25 miles final length having progressed at an average of 1½ miles per year and exactly 40 years after the first Act for a railway to Cardigan had been sought. The W. & C.R.'s arrival at Cilgerran put an end to the anachronistic use of boats on the river Teifi to take slate to Cardigan for shipment, enabling slate working in that village to survive into the 1930s. More importantly it ensured the survival of Cardigan itself as a trading centre after the detritus from the Teifi slate quarries had seriously silted up the port.

Shortly before he ceased to operate Cefn quarry (SN205429) in 1921, Captain Robert Hoare whose banking family effectively owned Oakeley quarry at Blaenau

Ffestiniog, planned a connection to the railway but overtaken by the collapse of the slate market the following year, his successors did not carry this out.

All this time, despite forming a natural route into Wales from the English Midlands, the Tanat valley a traditional area of slate and lead production, had no railway. At its eastern end the coal and limestone around Llanymynech made that village something of a railway centre yet almost every one of the many plans to lay metal west from there failed.

From 1845 lines such as the Worcester & Portdinlaen Railway, planned to pass along it, as did the West Midlands, Shrewsbury and Welsh Coast Railway, which in 1860, sought to combine coastal aims with tapping the riches of Blaenau, by tunnelling north-west from the Tanat valley to the Dee valley. Similar ambitions in 1864 of the Potteries, Shrewsbury & North Wales Railway, came to a grinding halt at Llanymynech.

Rails were laid west of Llanymynech in 1865, but thanks to the intervention of the citizens of Llanfyllin, they ran to that town along the pastoral Cain valley, rather than serving the slate and lead of the Tanat. This line incidentally proved counterproductive in that it facilitated access to Oswestry mart, to the detriment of the long-established Llanfyllin market.

It was only after the passing of the Light Railways Act of 1896, which enabled, subject to speed and other restrictions, a passenger railway to operate to less stringent standards than a 'full' railway, that a line was actually built. The standard gauge **Tanat Valley Light Railway** opened in 1904, running for just under 15 miles from the Cambrian line at Porthywaen near Llanymynech to Llangynog, it represented the culmination of 40 years of argument as to route. One early scheme had been for a narrow gauge line from Welshpool to Llanfair Caereinion which would then swing north, hacking through hill and dale to Llangynog (this line was partly built in 1903 as the 2' 6" gauge Welshpool and Llanfair Light Railway). Another idea was to do the opposite, striking northerly from Porthywaen, reaching Llangynog via Llansilin, yet another tried to do much the same thing making its way cross country from Oswestry. Among other schemes, of various gauges, was one to extend the Llanfyllin branch by tunnelling into the Tanat valley, another to do the same thing by crazily climbing over the mountain. There were also ideas of running a narrow gauge line to the tiny Cwmmaengwynedd slate quarry (SJ075326) and to the mines at Pistyll Rhaeadr.

In the end, as was so often the case, the route chosen was the obvious and easiest one, straight up the valley alongside the river. In spite of a minimum of engineering and having no branches, it took five years to build, although it has been alleged that the contractor delayed completion so that he could run unauthorised services on his own account!

It was a quaint line which in spite of its meanderings seemingly deliberately maximising the distance between most of its nine intermediate stations and the villages they served, it was for several decades a valuable link to the communities of the valley. Had it come say thirty years before its eventual opening date, Llangynog might well have become an important mining and quarrying centre. As it was, it came precisely when the whole slate industry was following lead mining into terminal decline.

The only mineral customer to be directly connected was Craig Rhiwarth quarry (SJ053263) which extended its incline to an exchange siding at Llangynog station.

Planned in the year the Tanat opened, was yet another of the great 'might-have-beens', the Penmachno, Corwen and Betws-y-coed Light Railway, which was the last of several bids to bring rails to south-west Denbighshire and substantially followed the route of part of the original North

Wales Narrow Gauge Railway plans. This line, also narrow gauge was to run from an exchange on the G.W.R. at Corwen and follow the Holyhead road in a stiff climb with grades up to 1 in 31, passing through a 166 yard tunnel and a 470 yard tunnel before descending to Cerrigydrudion. With grades up and down as steep as 1 in 25 the Conwy valley would be reached, there would be a further 153 yard tunnel before Moss Hill two miles short of Betws-y-coed. Here there was to be a branch up the Machno valley to Cwm Machno quarry (SH751470). Beyond here the grades would be eased by a loop, a 50 yard and a 387 yard tunnel, before the line burrowed under the Holyhead road. It would then have swung back on a big 180 degree loop to bridge the Llanrwst road, the river and the L. & N.W.R. to arrive at an interchange at what is now Betws-y-coed station car park. The Snowdon & Betws-y-coed Light Railway would have joined on the loop. This line also followed a proposed N.W.N.G. route but instead of the switch-backs at the head of Nant Gwynant, it was to tunnel through to Capel Curig and thence to Betws-y-coed. Had it been built, it would have ended the forty year wait for rail connection of Rhos (SH729564), Hafodlas (SH779562) and Hafod y Llan (SH613524) quarries, as well as encouraging the development of Bryn Engan (SH716569). Although with established slate handling facilities at Betws station, it is unlikely that this traffic would have used the P.C.& B.

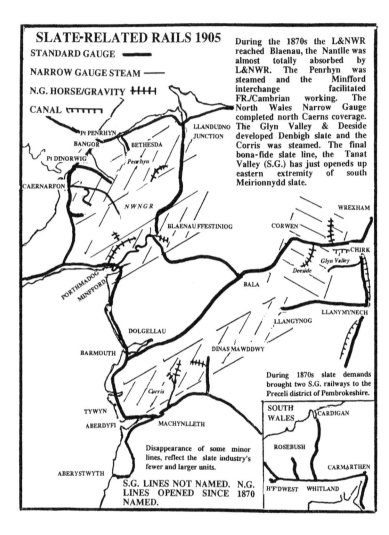

SLATE-RELATED RAILS 1905

STANDARD GAUGE ━━━

NARROW GAUGE STEAM ───

N.G. HORSE/GRAVITY ++++

CANAL ⊏⊐⊐⊐⊐⊓

During the 1870s the L&NWR reached Blaenau, the Nantlle was almost totally absorbed by L&NWR. The Penrhyn was steamed and the Minfford interchange facilitated FR./Cambrian working. The North Wales Narrow Gauge completed north Caerns coverage. The Glyn Valley & Deeside developed Denbigh slate and the Corris was steamed. The final bona-fide slate line, the Tanat Valley (S.G.) has just openeds up eastern extremity of south Meirionnydd slate.

Pt PENRHYN

BANGOR BETHESDA

Pt DINORWIG Penrhyn

CAERNARFON

LLANDUDNO JUNCTION

NWNGR

WREXHAM

BLAENAU FFESTINIOG CORWEN

CHIRK

Glyn Valley

Deeside

PORTHMADOG

MINFFORD

BALA

LLANYMYNECH

DOLGELLAU

LLANGYNOG

BARMOUTH

DINAS MAWDDWY

During 1870s slate demands brought two S.G. railways to the Preceli district of Pembrokeshire.

Corris

TYWYN

ABERDYFI MACHYNLLETH

SOUTH WALES CARDIGAN

ROSEBUSH

Disappearance of some minor lines, reflect the slate industry's fewer and larger units.

CARMARTHEN

ABERYSTWYTH

S.G. LINES NOT NAMED. N.G. LINES OPENED SINCE 1870 NAMED.

H'F'DWEST WHITLAND

11. The Twentieth Century. The Last Flourish

The twentieth century brought one final slate-related railway to Wales, the **Welsh Highland Railway** which although never a significant slate carrier, had its origins and aims very much rooted in the slate industry.

During the last thirty years or so of the 19th century, there had been a number of plans to build railways to or through Beddgelert. This village was strategically situated at the confluence of the Gwynant and Colwyn rivers with several copper mines and more than a dozen slate quarries in its vicinity. As early as the 1850s great potential was being ascribed to these small slate workings, the area being confidently predicted to become the 'New Penrhyn'. Although every plan to make railway connection had come to naught, whenever a slate digging around Beddgelert had been offered for sale, the particulars invariably stated that 'railway connection was imminent'.

Beddgelert had been one objective of the North Wales Narrow Gauge Railway, but by 1879 it had become obvious that they would not be building their Nant Gwynant line eastwards from Beddgelert, nor would they be making any input into the Croesor & Portmadoc Railway or its extension plan. In spite of the slate market now being in recession, the C. & P.R. re-invented itself as the Portmadoc, Croesor & Beddgelert Tram Railway and sought to implement the Garreg Hylldrem-Beddgelert Extension Plan.

This having failed to find backers, the Portmadoc & Beddgelert Railway was promoted in 1882, which in spite of the obvious economies of narrow gauge and of utilising the under-employed Croesor track, aimed to rehash part of Savin's abortive 1860s standard gauge Beddgelert Railway. Like that original scheme it was to continue the Beddgelert siding, but would only run up the eastern side of the

Aberglaslyn pass. Unsurprisingly, in view of the worsening state of the slate trade support was not forthcoming.

By the late 1880s, the slate trade was recovering strongly, and once more railway ideas flowed abundantly, mostly narrow gauge and mostly based on linking the Croesor with the N.W.N.G.R.

The Beddgelert & Rhyd Ddu Railway of 1890 was such a line. Making an end on junction with the N.W.N.G.R. at Rhyd Ddu, it would cross to the south of the road to serve Llyn y Gadair quarry (SH564519), and after turning south at Pitt's head to cross the Afon Cwm Ddu, it would descend to Beddgelert, restricting grades to a maximum of 1 in 40 by means of a series of 3 chain radius loops. Having passed behind the Royal Goat hotel it would cross the Glaslyn to the south of Beddgelert. To meet it on the east side of the river, the P.C. & B.T.R. would again revive their 1879 Extension Plan from Garreg Hylldrem. In 1892 the two lines were offered as a package as the Portmadoc, Beddgelert & Rhyd Ddu Railway, but still found no backers.

In 1898, taking advantage of the Light Railways Act, the P.B. & R.D.R. was again unsuccessfully trotted out as the Portmadoc, Beddgelert & Rhyd Ddu Light Railway. Its route from Rhyd Ddu was unchanged but south of Beddgelert it was to cross the Glaslyn about ¼ mile further downstream, and after going through a 280 yard tunnel, would re-cross the Glaslyn and run down its western side to Porthmadog station, ignoring the Croesor altogether.

By the turn of the century the market for slate was again weak, but the Penrhyn quarry dispute of 1900-1903 caused a temporary shortage of product. It was in this illusion of boom that in 1901 the Portmadoc, Beddgelert and South Snowdon Railway appeared on the scene. They planned to run an electric railway from Mount Pleasant, west of Morfa Bychan to Borth-y-gest and around the bay to tunnel through to the Porthmadog slate quays. This section being presumably intended, like the tramways at Pwllheli and at

Fairbourne, to promote housing development.

Having bought the Croesor line, they would use it as far as Garreg Hylldrem and run along the eastern side of the Aberglaslyn by three tunnels of 300, 17 and 37 yards. Swinging east opposite Beddgelert it would follow the river along Nant Gwynant, running to the south of the road to Pont Bethania, where it would cross the road and continue past Llyn Gwynant to a hydro-electric station which would supply the power. An end on junction was to be made with the proposed Snowdon & Betws-y-coed Light Railway, which was a rehash of the N.W.N.G.R. 1870s proposal.

In 1903, the P.B. & S.S.R. was bought by the newly – formed North Wales Power & Electric Traction Co. Primarily interested in promoting hydro-electric power, the railway company was probably only bought to gain the land acquisition rights implicit in a Railway Act. Even so they pressed on with the P.B. & S.S.R.'s ambitions. To connect with the N.W.N.G.R. they proposed the P.B. & S.S. Light Railway Extension. This would cross the Glaslyn and the Beddgelert-Tremadog road and after passing through a 43 yard tunnel behind the Royal Goat hotel, would climb to Pitt's head by a route which their electric traction would permit to be steeper and less sinuous than the 1890s schemes. At Pitt's Head it would cross to the Beddgelert-Caernarfon road and run to the north of it to make an end on junction with the N.W.N.G.R. at Rhyd Ddu.

Unlike the various previous schemes the P.B. & S.S.R. actually did some construction, cutting the Aberglaslyn tunnels and building trackbed to the north and south of them. The high clearance in the three tunnels is said to be due to the P.B. & S.S.R.'s need to provide clearance for overhead power wires, but actually the 'long' tunnel was only partly cut by the P.B. & S.S.R. and raising the height of all three was included in the W.H.R.'s 1920s list of works.

Almost all of the formation from Rhyd Ddu to Beddgelert was completed including the tunnel, an arched bridge over the road, the flanking walls of an accommodation bridge for a field route and the abutments of a river bridge opposite Beddgelert church.

In 1906 the N.W.P. & E.T. acquired the N.W.N.G.R., although they seem to have been directing its affairs since 1904 when they revived the old N.W.N.G.R. hopes of reaching Caernarfon. This was to be achieved either by persuading the L. & N.W.R. to make their Dinas-Caernarfon section three rail or by laying a new line from Dinas partly utilising the abandoned sections of the Nantlle tramway, including the Coed Helen tunnel, which would run onto a new quay on the south-west bank of the Seiont at Caernarfon.

Also in 1906, in spite of intending to be an electric railway which in any case had no permanent way of its own, the P.B. & S.S.R. actually took delivery of a steam locomotive. (This loco, 'Russell', a 2-6-2- Hunslet, served the N.W.N.G.R. and the Welsh Highland and after many vicissitudes it has finally returned to the W.H.R. [1964] at Porthmadog.) The P.B. & S.S.R. did not enjoy their new acquisition for long, since later the same year lack of funds brought the whole project to a standstill, and in 1908 they officially wound up. Bruce, Peebles & Co. Ltd. of Edinburgh who were the main contractors had commenced construction of 10 Ganz Patent electric locomotives, highly advanced machines designed for polyphase 660v AC current, two phases coming from overhead wires, the third from the track itself. When the P.B. & S.S.R. failed Bruce Peebles had six almost complete and their inability to find a buyer contributed to their own fall into receivership a few months later.

A search for someone to finance the completion of the line dragged on until the beginning of WW1 when some use was made of the Rhyd Ddu-Beddgelert formations for Government forestry work using temporary track, and it is reported, a De Winton locomotive.

In the meantime in 1913, with slate shipments at Porthmadog little more than a third of their 1873 peak, the general coastal trade in decline, and with a mere three seagoing fishing boats registered, compared with almost a dozen in the late 1890s, the Port Trustees were seeking a Treasury grant to upgrade the harbour to accept larger vessels. They backed their application with optimistic trade forecasts including predictions that a railway to Beddgelert would bring substantial additional slate business to the port. It was also visualised that exports of butter, poultry, eggs and even sugar beet and tobacco might be developed. Their submission also mentioned shipbuilding, although sadly the Gestiana then being completed would prove to be the final Porthmadog vessel. The re-siting of the sluices would have allowed the development of an inner harbour, in what was basically a revival of the Aberystwyth & Welch Coast Railway's scheme of half a century before.

The F.R. whose traffic had been halved in a decade, backed the proposal, their input included the revival of the 1901 Portmadoc, Beddgelert & South Snowdon idea of extending from the Porthmadog slate quays beyond Borth-y-gest. Unlike the P.B. & S.S.R. scheme they seem to have foreseen the extension serving agriculture and industry rather than housing.

The war put an end to any possibility of rejuvenating small harbours such as Porthmadog, but did not end railway ambitions, which were re-kindled in the euphoria of the post-war slate boom.

By this time the North Wales Power and Electric Traction Company besides owning the N.W.N.G.R. also effectively controlled the Ffestiniog Railway. With this combination and aided by substantial grants, they set about building the Welsh Highland Railway, which by linking the N.WN.G.R. with the Croesor, in effect extended the F.R. from Porthmadog to Dinas.

Track on the by now almost moribund N.W.N.G.R. was

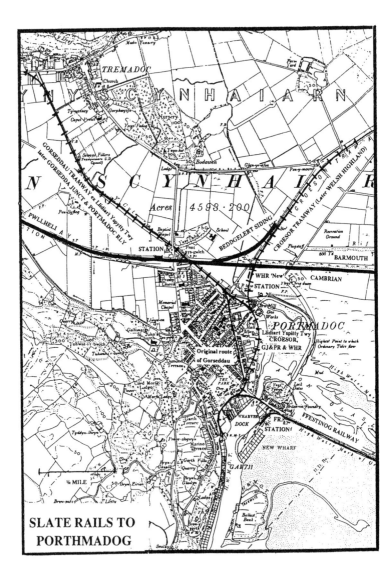

SLATE RAILS TO
PORTHMADOG

renewed. Just one locomotive was bought, an ex War Department 4-6-0 Baldwin, the rest of the stock being ex-N.W.N.G.R. items – some almost 50 years old!

To reach Beddgelert from Rhyd Ddu (which they renamed South Snowdon), part use was made of the P.B. & S.S. formations, but in descending from Pitts head the loops which had figured in the 1890s schemes were reintroduced to moderate the gradients. At Beddgelert the P.B. & S.S. proposed route across the Glaslyn was abandoned in favour of a downstream crossing to reach the part-constructed formations on the east bank and utilising them, a junction was made with the Croesor line near Garreg Hylldrem at what would be named Croesor Junction.

The Croesor was relaid between Garreg Hylldrem and Porthmadog and bridges rebuilt. Immediately on the town side of its crossing of the Cambrian main line, a station, Portmadoc New, offered a passenger interchange, the station building oddly situated at a lower level than the track. Where the line crossed the present High Street at Porthmadog an additional track was laid to make the junction triangular to allow through running by F.R. trains coming across the Cob.

The perennial plans for a line up Nant Gwynant were finally abandoned, and any ideas for running through to Caernarfon were not seriously pursued. The line continued what was becoming a slate railway tradition of being completed just when its traffic vanished, by opening in 1923 at the very end of the post-war slate boom. Even so, moderate tonnages continued to come from the quarries on the Bryngwyn branch, this traffic being the mainstay of the whole system. On the old N.W.N.G.R. main line virtually all the quarries had closed or were on the point of doing so, leaving only Garreg Fawr (SH538582) and Rhos Clogwyn (SH576530) to supply trifling tonnages. The surviving Croesor Tramway quarries, Rhosydd (SH664461) and Croesor (SH657457) would shortly fade into oblivion.

Ironically, of all the slate diggings in the Beddgelert area, which had been the prime cause of fifty years of railway ambition, not one remained in commercial operation. There were hopes of business from the Cwmbychan copper mine at Nanmor, but this proved a failure. With motor lorries becoming commonplace, there was scant general goods traffic and heavy freight traffic consisted mainly of occasional shunts at Porthmadog in and out of Glaslyn foundry, the Flour mill and Richard William's North Wales Slate Works, and the odd truck of coal finding its way to Beddgelert.

Having opened just when motor buses were, like motor lorries, becoming an established part of rural life, and having a population catchment of at most 3000, its non-tourist passenger traffic was at best trifling. For several years prior to its 1936 closure it virtually hibernated during the winter months.

It was the only Welsh railway to operate a dining car, which with a route mileage (including the Ffestiniog) of 35, this was perhaps a recognition of the actual as opposed to the timetabled, journey times!

Their motive power inventory was mixed. They had the 0-6-4 Moel Tryfan, one of the N.W.N.G.R's original single Fairlies, the redoubtable Russell and the Baldwin, later they also had a Kerr Stuart Diesel, possibly the first i.c. loco on a narrow gauge passenger line, unusually this was also a 'six wheeler'. In addition various Ffestiniog engines were used.

This rather sad, fifty-years-too-late, railway staggered bravely from crisis to crisis, its main economic impact being the highly negative one which it made on the F.R. balance sheet particularly from 1934 when the F.R. fully leased it.

It is to be hoped that the Millennium reincarnation of the W.H.R. will enjoy greater success.

12. The Twentieth Century and Road Transport

For the Welsh slate industry the first seventy years of the 20th century was, apart from brief respites following the two World Wars, a period of almost continuous decline. At the same time road transport took an increasing share of these diminishing outputs.

Steam traction engines had been used in the second half of the 19th century, probably the first was the one used by Glynrhonwy Lower Quarry (SH565607), prior to its 1869 rail connection, to tow a trailer to the slate quays at Caernarfon. From about the same time, Craig Rhiwarth (SJ053263) was using one to reach the railhead at Llanymynech (later bought by Hafod y Llan [SH613524]) to take output to the Croesor Tramway. The speed of all mechanical vehicles being limited to a walking pace meant that they were scarcely faster than horse carts, and the damage caused to roads by their iron wheels made them seriously unpopular with Local Authorities. After 1896 when speeds of up to 12 mph were allowed, steam lorries with solid rubber tyres became a proposition for producers such as Cwm Machno (SH751470), for their nine mile road journey to Betws-y-coed station.

By the 1900s, motor lorries, chiefly Continental imports, such as Milnes-Daimler were appearing, but prior to WW1 their cost, unreliability and to some extent the shortage of 'chauffeurs', restricted their use. In any case, lack of power, solid tyres, doubtful brakes, poor roads, oil or at best acetylene lamps, repeated breakdowns, and the 12 mph speed limit meant that cross-country journeys could take days. Hostelries being deeply reluctant to accommodate oily-overalled drivers and mates, often the only overnight shelter available to them was on the road underneath their cabless lorries. All this effectively limited motor transport to short hauls, posing little threat to the railways.

During WW1 there was little slate for the slate lines to carry but several were actively engaged in forestry work and some such as the Hendre Ddu, the North Wales Narrow Gauge and the Corris, laid additional track to meet this need.

After the war the ready availability of surplus military motor lorries and of ex-servicemen able to drive and maintain them, promoted their wider use. An indigenous motor lorry industry which had evolved to meet wartime demands switched to civilian needs, producing vehicles which were increasingly practical and reliable.

During the 1920s road surfaces improved dramatically and pneumatic tyres, on which speeds of up to 20 mph were permitted, became available for heavy vehicles. This greatly encouraged the use of lorries for local work, although right up to WW2 road deliveries over long distances remained unusual.

The first slate quarry to completely abandon a railway-in-being was probably Llwyngwern (SH757045) which on re-opening in 1922 after war time closure, found the Corris Railway bridge over the Dulas too decayed to use, so they lorried to Machynlleth station. A further loss to the Corris came in 1925 when Braich Goch (SH748078) bought a steam lorry, also using it to deliver to Machynlleth.

In 1930 the Cambrian quarry (SJ189378) went over to road transport, although its effect on the Glyn Valley line was serious, it was not immediately terminal since by then their traffic came mainly from stone quarries.

The floundering Welsh Highland lost virtually all its slate business in 1933 when the three surviving quarries on the Bryngwyn branch, Cilgwyn (SH500540), Alexandra (SH519562) and its associated Moel Tryfan (SH515559), started to deliver to the L.M.S.R. at Penygroes by lorry, claiming this cut their costs of reaching the main line by two-thirds. The Croesor quarries having closed, this left the W.H.R. with just token quantities from Rhos Clogwyn

(SH576530).

It has been somewhat cynically said that in addition to cost savings, having ones own lorry avoided the risk of the railway distraining on consignments, if payments to them were in arrears!

At Blaenau, the Ffestiniog Railway lost out mainly not to road competition, but to the main line railways. In 1936 Llechwedd quarry which for years had been an almost 100% user of the F.R. and its mainstay customer, diverted almost all its output to the L.M.S.R. via the exchange sidings at Pantyrafon. The Oakeley quarry, in spite of having since 1930, a line from the Glan y Don tip straight into the L.M.S.R. yard, had remained more or less faithful to the F.R., but even they became exasperated with the F.R.'s shortcomings. The F.R.'s woes were exacerbated by the closure of the Groby granite quarry, the carrying of whose stone to the L.M.S.R. station had provided useful revenue.

The move towards road transport was reflected in the post WW1, 'greenfield' slate developments, all such as the small Cwmbach quarry (SH564406) of 1921, New Crown (SH513556) ten years later and the potentially important Marchlyn (SH602628), were sited without thought or need of rail connection. Added to which the availability of motor lorries enabled several remote diggings such as Nantglyn (SH978598) which had struggled with carts for a century or more, to be competitive. Similarly Rhos (SH729564) and Cwm Machno (SH751470) quarries, neither of which ever had rail connection, proved hardy survivors, closing in 1952 and 1962 respectively, due to manning problems, not transport difficulties. Likewise Clogau quarry (SJ185463) could soldier on (as it still does!) long after the Oernant tramway had fallen to bits.

In spite of attritions and forebodings, rail branches and feeder lines generally retained much of such slate traffic as there was up to WW2, their most serious losses being in passenger numbers.

At first motor buses had been seen not as competitors but as adjuncts to railways, and some of the earliest were operated by railway companies. Typical were the 1906 L. & N.W.R. Mold-Connahs Quay, and the Cambrian Pwllheli-Nevin services, as well as the motor bus excursions run by the Corris from 1908. In fact the first notable cessation of passenger services by the North Wales Narrow Gauge (Bryngwyn branch 1913 and main line 1916), was due to there being insufficient freight traffic to support timetabled services, not to road competition.

Post WW1 it was a different matter. As with lorries, ex-army drivers spent their gratuities on buying and converting ex-government vehicles, to start motor bus services. Some sought to serve villages lacking rail connection, but others competed head to head with the branch and feeder railways.

A Blaenau-Porthmadog bus service started in 1923, but the hammer blow to the F.R. came three years later when quarrymen angered by the loss of wages which the unreliability of the F.R. was causing them, persuaded Messrs Crossville to put on workmen's services.

The practicality of buses was dramatically boosted when the 1930 Road Traffic Act allowed them to travel at up to 30 mph, adding speed to the cost and convenience advantages they already offered. Additionally obtaining bus operators' permits was made easier and restrictions on railway companies doing so were relaxed. Within the year the Mawddwy had withdrawn passenger services, the Llanberis branch was only running tourist trains and the F.R. had ceased winter passenger services. The G.W.R. who had taken over the Corris, replaced passenger trains with buses (sacking the firemen and the crossing keepers at Garnedd-wen, Llwyngwern and Ffridd Gate).

In 1933 passenger traffic ended on the Glyn Valley line as did winter running on the Welsh Highland. Passenger trains ceased on the W.H.R. in 1936, but by aggressive marketing the F.R. retained and increased their tourist numbers, but trying to cover most of 12 months costs with about 6 weeks' revenue, was 'no way to run a railway', and with war ending tourism, passenger services finished in 1939.

Cessation of passenger trains had a knock-on effect upon the parcels traffic which they carried. This work was taken over by motor vans, which the 1930 Act also allowed to travel at 30 mph. Added to which the railways began to phase out their horse drays thus opening the way for goods deliveries to be made from main line depots rather than from branch line stations.

In 1935, the effect of the motor bus not only on competitive forms of travel but also on the social structure of the slate districts was presaged when the health authority ordered the closure of the Anglesey barracks at Dinorwig quarry. A bus service was put on which enabled the dispossessed occupants to live at home, their daily journey incidentally taking about an hour instead of the erstwhile weekly four hour walk/boat/train/epic.

Motor fuel rationing during and for seven years following WW2 halted the drift of traffic to the roads, but with slate working at a low ebb, there was little business for either road or rail. The Ffestiniog Railway in its original form, stumbled through WW2 on an 'as required' basis, closing in 1946 when its monthly tonnage barely reached 700. Just a short stretch, the top end of the Duffws branch and the connection to the L.M.S.R. station (shortly to be B.R., Blaenau North) remained in use to handle Maenofferen, Diffwys and Bowydd output. The Corris managed to stagger on until 1948 when the Dyfi bridge was flood-damaged and there were no funds to repair it.

Lines such as the Croesor had withered when their quarry customers closed. However, the Penrhyn, Dinorwig and what was left of the Nantlle continued to function.

The standard gauge lines, shored up by subsidies, generally fared remarkably well, nearly all surviving until the 'Beeching cuts' of the 1960s. Almost the only exceptions

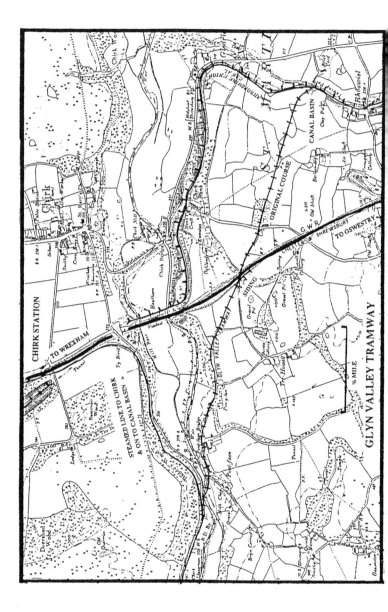

being the very lightly used Mawddwy line which closed in 1950 and the Bala-Ffestiniog which succumbed to reservoir construction in 1961.

Although the lines survived, the traffic did not. The ending of road fuel rationing in 1952, the denationalisation of heavy haulage, the liberalisation of both the commercial vehicle licensing system and speed limits, together with road improvements including the commencement of motorway building, slashed the railway's share of freight traffic.

The same factors also finally ended coastwise shipment of both slate and other cargoes.

As early as 1947 the Padarn's workmen's trains ceased. The now diminished Dinorwig workforce having long discovered that buses could pick them up in their home villages and if required, deliver them at mills level half way up the quarry. Only four years later the Penrhyn also ended workmen's travel.

These two lines hung on as slate carriers until economic realities brought closure in 1961 and 1962 respectively.

Simultaneously the ports' standard gauge rail connections also closed. Both Port Dinorwig and Port Penrhyn for a time survived this loss of rail connection, occasional export cargoes, brought in by road continuing to be shipped at both ports for another decade.

At Blaenau in 1962 the last cargo (from Maenofferen) went out through what was left of the Duffws branch and in 1964, Llechwedd ceased sending trucks down its incline for loading onto the Ex-L.M.S.R. line. At the end of the decade, Oakeley closed ending the use of their now much improved Glan y Don link.

By this time the motor car was proving even more successful than the motor bus in capturing railway passenger traffic for all but the longest journeys. Goods sent by rail increasingly suffered losses, delays and mis-deliveries, which together with high charges led to the

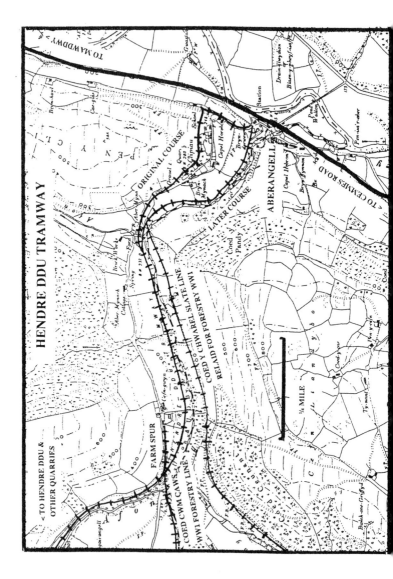

HENDRE DDU TRAMWAY

TO MAWDDWY >

ABERANGELL

< TO CEMMES ROAD

ORIGINAL COURSE

LATER COURSE

COED Y CHWAREL SLATE LINE
RELAID FOR FORESTRY WWI

WWI FORESTRY LINE

COED CWM CAWS

FARM SPUR

< TO HENDRE DDU &
OTHER QUARRIES

¼ MILE

further diminution of rail's share of every kind of freight. In reality, the 'Beeching Axe' of the mid 1960s was regrettably inevitable.

By now, slate production was tumbling, few quarries were working and their output bordered on the insignificant. Thus although the 1960s saw two thirds of Welsh track mileage lifted, the only surviving quarry to be deprived of direct rail connection was Penyrorsedd (SH510538), which had continued to use the horse-drawn rump of the Nantlle Railway until B.R. closed it in 1963. The only other surviving major quarry on the Nantlle, Dorothea (SH500532) having given up its use almost ten years earlier, when rails were also abandoned for internal movement.

Although Dorothea's foresight and enterprise were unable to stave off its 1970 closure, its example was followed by others and by the late 1970s rail tracks were only to be found in underground workings. Since almost all extraction was by now opencast, only Maenofferen and Aberllefenni (SH768103) retained their rails.

The recovery which occurred in the industry during the 1980s was entirely based on rough-terrain lorries, diggers, etc. Maenofferen even used a small digger underground. The cessation of work at that quarry in 1998, left Aberllefenni quarry the only user of railed wagons and its Clayton battery loco a unique survivor.

In spite of its contribution to the truncation of the railway network, even the most dedicated railway apologist could not deny the many positive benefits of the motor car. Apart from the general ones of broadening horizons and enriching people's lives, in Wales within a slate connotation there have been especial social benefits. Widespread car ownership has ensured the survival of communities such as Croesor, Corris, Talysarn and the biblically named villages of north Caernarfonshire, which would otherwise have decayed once their life-blood of slate quarrying had been withdrawn. In addition, although many of the isolated dwellings self-built by quarrymen on the hillsides in the Caernarfon hinterland and to a lesser extent on the southern flanks of the Preselau, have fallen into ruin, a number, thanks to the motor car, have not.

13. Routes and Remains

Generally feeder tramways are defined from their remoter ends, railway branches from their junctions. Gauges quoted are nominal.

ABEREIDDI TRAMWAY (SM795315 to 813325. 3'g. Horse) *c.1850-1890s.*
The initial length from the engine house at Abereiddi quarry was lost during an early 1900s attempt to create a harbour. However several hundred yards make an obvious path past various buildings including worker's cottages (Abereiddi Terrace), and a fine powder house. From there on almost to Porthgain it is less evident.

ARTHOG TRAMWAY (SH651152 to 648156. 2'g. Horse/gravity) *c.1858-1868 (possible later use).*
The abutments of the bridge which carried the line over the road to the mill area which is now a caravan site, is obvious. From here on both the early route to the jetty and the newer one to the railway are clearly defined. The former line goes through a rock archway.

BALA – BLAENAU BRANCH G.W.R. (SH936355 to 701459. S.G.) *1882– Closed Passengers 1960; Freight 1961. (Bala Junction to Bala open to 1965). Trawsfynydd to Blaenau retained and connection made through to the Llandudno Junction-Blaenau line to service Trawsfynydd power station.*
The Bala Junction-Bala section has been largely lost, Bala station now redeveloped. From Bala the trackbed may be followed almost continuously to the Tryweryn dam with some buildings and trackside features intact. It emerges at the far end of the lake from where it is well defined, with some trace of the stone crusher plant at Arenig (SH830392), until at the summit it is partly absorbed in road widening. From there through a cutting and across the viaduct

(SH776387) much of its spectacular route, partly carved from almost vertical cliffs, can be walked.

The relatively extensive Trawsfynydd station and goods yard is now an agricultural supplies depot. As at the military station some 200 yards further north west, the platform is intact. From Trawsfynydd to the power station the route is obvious, with at least one accommodation bridge extant. The power station depot and gantry is on the site of Trawsfynydd Lake Halt.

Recent work has obscured much of Maentwrog Road station, and Teigl Halt has vanished, but traces remain of Llan Ffestiniog and Manod stations, just beyond the latter are vestiges of the spur which curved around the cemetery and through 180 degrees to Madog roadstone quarry (SH708448), gates and the gated gap where two houses were demolished denote where the line crossed the road. Tan y Manod yard exchange for Graig Ddu and (due to shortage of space at Blaenau), the site of the turntable and engine shed, are referred to in the Festiniog & Blaenau entry.

Much of the site of the Blaenau station (Blaenau Ffestiniog Central in B.R. days), is occupied by the present S.G./N.G. joint station. The large goods shed has gone as have the extensive goods sidings and the interlocking S.G./N.G. transfer lines. The headshunt extended to just east of the Dorvil Bridge (opposite the Market Hall), roughly on the line of the present F.R. It is fitting, in view of the prominent part that railways such as this played in education, that part of the station site is occupied by Maenofferen school.

BANGOR – CAERNARFON BRANCH (SH547707 to 481632. S.G.) *1852 – closed Passengers 1970; Freight 1972.*
The road and other works have obliterated most of the trackbed near where it left the Holyhead main line, and beyond the Vaynol tunnel it is absorbed by the Port Dinorwig by-pass. Near and into Caernarfon much is

traceable to the site of the town station (now Safeway supermarket).

BETHESDA BRANCH (SH585712 to 618668. S.G.) *1884 – closed Passengers 1951; Freight 1953.*
Most of the trackbed from its junction (facing from Bangor) just west of the Cegin bridge is obvious and is passable except where it has been cut by roadworks, following the south bank of the Cegin as far as Glasinfryn. Little remains of the seven arched viaduct over the river, the skew bridge over the Penrhyn Railway or the bridge over the B4366. After passing under the Tregarth road it is briefly traceable alongside the Penrhyn Railway formation. At Tregarth there are two further underbridges and deep in a cutting, another bridge takes it under both a road and the Penrhyn Railway before entering the 300 yard Tregarth tunnel. There are traces of the five arch span over the Ogwen where it emerged from the tunnel, beyond which there is a fairly well defined run to the site of Bethesda station.

BLAENAU BRANCH L. & N.W.R./L.M.S.R. (SH800777 to 697461. S.G.) *1879 –*
Still in use and very much unchanged from its original construction apart from the usual obliteration of redundant structures, notably at Betws-y-coed where all trace of the extensive sidings have vanished. Also gone are the sidings at Dolwyddelan station which made Ty'n y Bryn (SH742521) one of the very few slate quarries to have direct standard gauge rail connection. Further on an interesting relic is the trackbed of the 3' gauge tramway which ran from SH700487 to 689501 laid by contractor Gethin Jones to facilitate construction of the Moel Dyrnogydd tunnel. It is said that its routing through his slate quarry at SH696496 was entirely fortuitous!

All trace of the original passenger station to the east of the line at the tunnel portal at Pantyrafon was obliterated by the building of the Llechwedd exchange sidings and yard, of which a crane and storage sheds remain flanked by the Llechwedd hydro-electric station. On the opposite side are the vestiges of the corresponding exchange arrangements for Oakeley quarry. From here complex bridging enables the line to cross and re-cross the Barlwyd.

The main passenger building of Blaenau station (Blaenau Ffestiniog North in B.R. days), has gone, but a subsidiary building remains, as does one platform and part of the decoratively-bricked wall of the station approach ramp. The goods and the narrow gauge-standard gauge exchange areas are part-occupied by a fire station, a bus depot etc. but there is no trace of the goods shed or the fine four-road engine shed. Although the Glan y Don tip has been levelled, the margin for the 1930 2′ gauge line from its incline to the station shows up on the inside of the curve of the line into the station site and the abutments of the bridge over Glan y Pwll road are extant alongside the standard gauge bridge.

The route of the extension to the new Blaenau station follows the line of the old narrow gauge connection from the F.R. Duffws branch.

At Deganwy (SH782788, on the Llandudno Junction-Llandudno branch) much of the wharfage is extant and the layout of both the standard gauge and the narrow gauge tracks can be deduced. Movement on the latter was by capstan and rope.

CAERNARFON – AFON WEN BRANCH (SH481632 to 445372. S.G.) *1868-1964.*
Streets and the tunnel define the route from the town station to the Slate Quays approach, from where as far as Dinas the trackbed has been re-used for the 2′ gauge Welsh Highland Railway revival. The road approximately defines the route of the branch to the slate quays, which are now a car park. The route is readily traceable past Penygroes much of the way to Afon Wen, most is now a cycle track.

CARNARVONSHIRE SLATE QUARRIES RAILWAY
(SH491523 to 481529. 3' 6"g. Horse) *c.1850s – c.1915.*

Just traceable from Tan yr Allt quarry with a bridge under a road. Past possible connections to other workings to vestiges of a river bridge. Curving to the west it rises to meet the Nantlle (later S.G.) at what is now a road at SH481529.

CEDRYN TRAMWAY (SH702637 to 781668. 2'g. Horse)
c.1861-1880s.

From Cwm Eigiau quarry to near Cedryn quarry is a rough path. From Cedryn to the head of the three pitch incline down to the valley floor most of the trackbed is now a road, except at the Pwll Ddu incline (SH745664) where the road follows the route of the standard gauge line put in during the building of the Cwm Eigiau reservoir in 1907.

Trace of the lowest pitch of the big incline was lost when the whole was straightened into a single-pitch haulage for the reservoir construction. This new uphaulage was also used from 1917 to 1968 to reach the 2' gauge Colwyd railway which ran off southwards from its head. The hut for the haulage engine is extant. This incline also carries the pipes which power the Dolgarrog aluminium works, the building of which obscured the run of the line to the river.

CHWAREL FEDW TRAMWAY (SH748525 to 744528. 2'g. Horse?) *1840s? – 1880s.*

From the quarry, the much degraded incline passes under the railway. An embanked formation takes it to the northern side of the valley, crossing the river by a fine, partly rebuilt bridge.

CORRIS, MACHYNLLETH & RIVER DYFI TRAMWAY
(SH770098 to SN710995. 2' 3"g. Horse) *1859-1879.*
CORRIS RAILWAY (SH770098 to 745015. 2' 3"g. Steam)
1879 – Passengers to 1930, Goods 1948.

The Quarry Branch started at the Aberllefenni quarry adit, near the old quarry offices (SH769102) running alongside the road to the present Aberllefenni mill passing the abutments of the bridge which carried the Ratgoed line over it. In front of the mill was a complex of sidings from where the line rose to the station.

Although the site of Aberllefenni station building has been partly obscured by housing, cantilevered access steps make its location obvious. The route parallels the road, past the traces of the spur to Matthews Mill (SH768091). After it crosses to the south of the road at Garneddwen it can be followed across field to Corris. There some of the line has been built on but the river bridge still stands.

Corris station itself has been demolished but the stable (for the delivery van horses), now houses the Railway Museum. The Corris Railway Society has relaid ¾ mile of track to Maespoeth (SH754066), where the engine shed now serves as their engineering depot. In time it is hoped to extend a further 1¼ miles to Pantperthog. From Maespoeth, where the Upper Corris Tramway joined, almost to Machynlleth the route follows the road. The tiny Escairgeiliog and Llwyngwern stations have been rebuilt as bus shelters. Near each of these, spurs led to respectively, Escairgeiliog Mill (SH759059) and Llwyngwern quarry (SH757045). At the former, the wooden bridge lies wrecked in the river.

Shortly after crossing the Llanwrin road at what was Ffridd Gate station, the formation leaves the road and crosses fields to the vestiges of the Dyfi bridge (now replaced by a cycle bridge), whose collapse brought about the line's closure.

The station area immediately alongside Machynlleth station is now occupied by various industrial buildings, but the fine station and headquarters building is in re-use.

The tramway route south of Machynlleth station is defined by a bricked-up arch under the main line railway. From there it passes through a garage forecourt and can be traced through side streets and on intermittently, paralleling the railway to Derwen-las, where in the old port area just the public house (Tafarn Isa) and the harbourmaster's house survive. The river is now some distance away, having been diverted during the building of the railway. The line is traceable to its Quay Ward terminus, where it crossed the main line railway close to the present accommodation crossing. The houses now extant are reconstructions of lead mining dwellings and warehouses. A little further on there is a fragment of a wall which was part of a cottage belonging to Gaewern quarry. There is now no trace of the actual slate wharves. Leading on west from here is an embanked track which may have been associated both with shipbuilding and a ford to Penal at SN703996. Between Derwen-las and Quay Ward, the lower end of the Morben quarry incline has been obliterated by the road and the railway, but the fine powder house is still in sound condition at SN716995.

CROESOR TRAMWAY (SH654461 to 569385. 2'g. Horse) *1864-1930. South from SH608428 re-used by Welsh Highland Railway to 1937. Beddgelert siding lifted 1959. (Part re-used by W.H.R.1964 revival.)*
This is clearly traceable from the foot of the Rhosydd and Croesor inclines, down the Blaen y Cwm incline to a clapper bridge near the newly revived hydro station. The route forms a path along the valley floor, past the foot of the Fronboeth incline, which was originally a two pitch incline from Pantmawr quarry in the next valley at SH658446. It can be seen how the lower pitch was extended upwards, the upper pitch abandoned and a line running down valley was

benched out to a tunnel. This tunnel has fallen in but can be entered from the southern side where a tramway and incline come down from Fronboeth (SH652448) and Cefn y Braich (SH646448) quarries.

At Croesor village, land ownership forced the crossing and re-crossing of the river by two excellent clapper bridges.

Since this upper part of the line was never officially lifted, such rail and chairs which have not found secondary employment around Croesor village, remain on the ground.

At the village the branch from Parc Slab quarry (SH632444) curves in via a cutting and the line continues via a fine embankment to the head of the Upper Parc incline, where the drumhouse has been rebuilt as a house, but the Lower Parc incline drumhouse is ruinous. At the foot of the inclines the Parc quarry branch joins from SH626436.

The formation, much of it embanked, crosses the flood plain and shortly after the site of the level crossing at Pont Garreg Hylldrem it swings southward and becomes much less well defined. Nearer Pont Croesor on the Garreg-Prenteg road it is more obvious and from there on it runs on an embankment to Porthmadog, which carries the track of the present 1964 Welsh Highland revival. Their rails leave the Croesor formation to utilise the trackbed of the 'Beddgelert' siding. The Croesor formation follows parallel as a footpath, past the present Welsh Highland Railway Gelert works (established by the Ffestiniog Railway, both to service the W.H.R. and to supplement Boston Lodge). Between this original formation and the re-used siding are vestiges of the exchange platform and remains of the weighbridge. The present W.H.R. Porthmadog car park occupies both the route of the Gorseddau line and the cattle yard of the main line railway.

The original crossing of the main line has been lost but beyond it the much overgrown formation curves south past what was the site of the W.H.R. 'Portmadoc New' station, of which only the water tower pillars remain, and on to the bridge across the Tremadog canal (Y Cyt). The formation which diverges to run to the intersection of Madoc Street and Madoc Street West marks a proposed but unused route. After crossing the canal all trace is lost but it did in fact swing around in front of the Porthmadog flour mill, now 'The Mill Shop', the mill being served by a loop not a siding. The revised route of the Gorseddau tramway (Gorseddau & Portmadoc Junction Railway) joined at this point and a couple of hundred yards was retained as a spur to reach the sidings of Richard Williams' North Wales Slate Works, now in industrial re-use, the spur (now defined by a lane) terminating at a monumental mason's yard.

The line crossed Snowdon Street to follow a curved path through what is now a large car park. A siding led into the Glaslyn Foundry, now the site of Leo's Stores. High street having been crossed almost at right angles the line continued on through what is now the Ffestiniog Railway car park, to join the wharf lines. When reused by the Welsh Highland, the route was connected to the Ffestiniog Railway by a line curving from the direction of the Cob. The Garreg-Hylldrem-Porthmadog section will eventually be incorporated into the revived W.H.R.

CWM EBOL TRAMWAY (SH689017 to SN703996. 3'/2' 3"g. Horse/gravity) *c.1868 – c.1900.*
Within the quarry area the line runs along the access road, turns right to drop down by incline and turns left to parallel the river. This probably superseded, or was superseded by, a route straight through the quarry area. The line is readily followed via an incline at SH695009 near which was a quartz mine which also used this tramway. After crossing the road, the course (which may have been a Roman road to a ford) is obvious to the wharf at Llyn Bwtri.

CWMORTHIN TRAMWAY (SH670466 to 685450. 2'g. Horse/Gravity) *1850-1939.*

From Conglog quarry mill its formation along the valley now partly forms a track. At Cwmorthin quarry there are vestiges of a short incline and on beyond, through a cutting, is a very fine two-pitch incline down to the F.R. at Tanysgrisiau.

DEESIDE TRAMWAY (SJ125400 to 152428. 2' 6"g. Horse/Gravity) *1870 (or before?) – 1947.*

Walkable from the foot of the exit incline at Moel Ferna quarry, via an incline at Deeside quarry (SJ138404) to the Nant y Pandy Mill (SJ148417) and on to the one-time office near the head of the incline at SJ149425, which carried it under the main road and on to Glyndyfrdwy station.

In places from Deeside mill to the head of incline fragments of wooden rail and iron gauge rods survive in situ.

DINORWIG RAILWAY (SH595605? to 527679. 2'"g. Horse) *1824-1843.*

Working has destroyed all vestiges at the quarry end, but the present road through Dinorwig village defines its route, continuing as a lane from Bigil (SH579622) to the head of the inclines. These two tandem pitches now form a path at the foot of which are the remains of stables. Roads mark the route through Clwb y Bont village as far as the former slate factories on either side of the road at SH574631. From there it is intermittently traceable to Efail Castell at SH565655, where at a loop in the road is the now rebuilt stable which survived as a general smithy until c. 1950. Beyond here, much of the trackbed is lost as far as the lane leading to Garth Fach (SH547679), where at the head of the Garth incline are possible tramway-related buildings. Little trace other than fragments of slate sleepers remain in the afforested area. Beyond this it is obliterated by subsequent railway and road works other than the north portal of the under-road tunnel. The final yards to the port are defined by a pathway running on the north-east side of the stream.

FESTINIOG & BLAENAU RAILWAY (SH704418 to 701459. 2'g. Steam) *1868-1882*.

Its trackbed was substantially occupied by the subsequent Bala-Ffestiniog G.W.R. branch and at Llan Ffestiniog the building of that branch has obliterated all trace of the F. & B.'s terminus (the site is now a garage), and much of the route.

Manod station at SH706452, was the loading point for slate brought down the Graig Ddu incline system. Known as Tan y Manod yard in G.W.R. days (Manod station then being ½ mile nearer Llan Ffestiniog), quarry trucks were loaded onto transporters to be taken to Blaenau. The area is now cleared leaving just vestiges of the slate loading bank but nothing of the G.W.R. turntable and engine shed. On the far side of the Afon Bowydd are traces of a writing slate factory.

The short incline down from road level which reversed back from the foot of the lower pitch of the Graig Ddu incline, has been obliterated by housing, as has a subsequent incline from Pengwern roadstone quarry (SH707450). The stocking yard at the foot of the Graig Ddu incline is in reuse as a scrap yard and the original connection to Pengwern quarry which joined at this point is traceable. All three extant pitches of the Graig Ddu incline are still a magnificent landscape feature.

Beyond Manod is the standard gauge masonry viaduct (which replaced the F. & B. wooden viaduct), behind it can be seen the shelf of the formation used during the original viaduct construction. At Blaenau, all relics belong to the G.W.R. era.

FFESTINIOG RAILWAY (SH702459 & 696468 to 569385. 2'g. Horse/Gravity) *1836-1863.* Steam. *1863 – closed passengers 1939, goods 1946, Duffws as feeder to B.R. 1962. (Reopened progressively from 1954 to 1982.)*

The Dinas branch provides some of the most interesting relics. Its start from the original Glan y Pwll triangular junction is traceable, except where encroached on by the Oakeley tips. The 1899 deviation has been re-railed as far as the first crossing of the Afon Barlwyd just short of Dinas station. At the station, the second Holland incline, like its predecessor which came down to the old triangular junction, as well as the hamlet of Tre'r Ddôl, have all been buried, but the 1905 Oakeley incline is extant as are the prominent zig-zag steps. There are vestiges of one station building and the old level crossing of the L. & N.W.R. standard gauge survives as a stile crossing. The bed of the freight-only route beyond the passenger station continues, nestling under the standard gauge, before finally diving under it to the foot of the Llechwedd quarry incline at Pantyrafon. Except for the removal of bridges this route has been preserved as a possible future tourist access to Llechwedd Caverns.

The original but now vanished, Welsh Slate Company's incline joined immediately before the line turned under the standard gauge. Its replacement is extant immediately north of the abutment of the Pen-y-Bont viaduct which led to the now removed Glan y Don tip. This tip provided additional tipping space for the Welsh Slate Company, and ultimately carried the Glan y Don mill. The 90' high Pen-y-Bont viaduct was built by the quarry carpenters in 1854, apparently copying Brunel designs. A spur off this incline (which still has track on the ground) curved tightly right, behind the viaduct pillar at a level slightly higher than the S.G. Wagons could then be reversed northwards, over the (still extant) bridge across the drain from the Oakeley Lefel Dŵr, to an extensive loading platform. A branch of the S.G. close to the tunnel mouth could accept both side loading and end loading. The trackbeds of this area remain, much overgrown. Partly due to awkwardness of operation this facility was little used, Oakeley traffic being worked to the L. & N.W.R. station via the link from the F.R. Duffws branch. This awkward working was replaced in 1930 by an incline down from the Glan y Don mill to a narrow gauge line which is traceable following alongside the curve of the S.G. to the L. & N.W.R. (later L.M.S.R.) station.

South of the viaduct abutment the original Mathew's incline and its spur line west of the river has been tipped over as has Rhiwbryfdir, an historic farm house.

The Duffws terminus is now a car park with the station building in reuse as a public convenience. The formations of both the Maenofferen/Rhiwbach No. 1 and the Diffwys/Bowydd inclines, are extant, the latter resurfaced as a path. Between them is the road which after 1962 gave access to Bowydd and Diffwys quarries and the foot of No. 2 incline (serving Maenofferen).

The Queen's bridge which carried Church Street over the tracks from Duffws station has been replaced by infill and site of the G.W.R./F.R. exchange platform which latterly served as the F.R. passenger terminus, is lost under the new station car park.

The present Blaenau Ffestiniog station shared with the standard gauge, approximately occupies the site of the G.W.R./F. & B. station (Blaenau Ffestiniog Central in B.R. days), the ex-L. & N.W.R./L.M.S. line reaching it approximately on the route of the 2' gauge which ran to the exchange sidings at the L. & N.W.R./L.M.S. station. The present F.R. line on the south side of the station is a new lay, approximately on the line of the F.R. branch which crossed the G.W.R. headshunt to run to the S.G./N.G. exchange and had a spur past Market Square to the Newborough slate mill (defined by lanes).

Past the traffic roundabout of the new Tanygrisiau road, there is scant trace of the old F.R. station (Stesion Fain) which allowed F.R. passengers to transfer to the L. & N.W.R. (L.M.S.R.) station. The canopy is in reuse as a stand at Manod football ground. Beyond Glan y Pwll level crossing the old F.R. engine shed has been rebuilt as a modern engineering depot.

Part way to Tanygrisiau, just beyond what was the Glan y Pwll triangular junction, a footbridge crosses the line at the site of the spur to the foot of the Nyth y Gigfran quarry incline. A little beyond, the 1908 branch to the Groby granite quarry is just traceable and near the present Tanygrisiau station (now on a new raised formation) is the foot of the lower incline of the Cwm Orthin branch. From here the present route diverges well to the north of the 1836 line which ran where the Visitor Centre now stands and continued along what is now the road to the power station. The 1852 route cut across the present reservoir on an embankment to the power station road. The foot of the Wrysgan incline was just where the road up to the upper dam now swings around the picnic area.

The power station cuts the old route, the Moelwyn incline cascade joining close by. Except where cut by the upper reservoir (Llyn Stwlan), its pitches still make a unique landscape feature.

When the reservoir level is low (generally in the morning when the water has been pumped up to Llyn Stwlan overnight), the old trackbed can be seen going towards the 'inlet' formed by the cutting at the north end of the 1842 Moelwyn tunnel. It is possible to make out traces of the feeder line from the Moelwyn copper mine at SH673438. Also at 'Low tide' the trackbed leading from near the tunnel mouth to a powder magazine and Brookes granite quarry at SH682438, is discernible.

The present Deviation route breaches the dam which powered the haulage incline, and later a mill belonging to Mathew's quarry (later the Gloddfa Ganol part of Oakeley), so sited because of the dearth of water-power at the quarry itself. The inclines of the 1836 'over the hump' route form a prominent path. The spoil heaps around the three tunnel air shafts are obvious. Once in sight of Dduallt station and the 'Alpine' loop of the Deviation, the now abandoned 1842 route to the southern end of the tunnel can be seen.

At SH658413 the short tunnel and its original route (up to 1863) around Garnedd rock is not easily reached, but it can be glimpsed by going through a sheep creep immediately up line from Tan y Bwlch station.

From here to Harbour Station at Porthmadog the line almost exactly conforms to the 1836 route. At the complex Minffordd interchange some F.R. track and all the standard gauge branch track has been lifted, but at Boston Lodge the layout is substantially unchanged. The network of lines both on the Cei Mawr, east of the Britannia bridge and along the quays west of it, have long since been lifted and built on.

FRON GOCH TRAMWAY (SN664973 to 664971. 2'g. Manpower) *c.1859-1884.*
This short line is obvious, emerging from a tunnel which gives access to the quarry pit. It crossed the road, past the small mill building to a now degraded stone jetty which was also one of the intended termini of the Corris, Machynlleth and River Dyfi Tramway.

GLYN VALLEY TRAMWAY (SJ202378 to 298368. 2' 4¼"g. Horse) *1873-1888* (SJ195351 to 284386. 2' 4½" g. Steam) *1888 – Passengers 1933, Freight 1935.*
Most of the roadside route on either side of Glynceiriog village has been lost to road widening, but where it departs from the road the route is obvious including a crossing and recrossing of the river. Equally obvious is the station area in the village where streets define the inclines down from the Cambrian and the Wynne quarries.

From Pontfaen paths and roads indicate but do not exactly define the original route to the canal wharf at

Gledrid bridge. The steamed line continued along the road beyond Pontfaen to SJ281372 where a path shows where it diverged. This can be partly traced to where it crossed over the canal tunnel to run to Chirk station and to the canal wharf immediately beyond, at the back of a modern factory.

GORSEDDAU TRAMWAY (SH571453 to 569385. 3'g. Horse) *1856 – c.1870.* **GORSEDDAU JUNCTION & PORTMADOC RAILWAYS** (SH541505 to 569385. 2'g. steam?) *1875 – c.1890.*
From the final terminus at the foot of the Blaen Pennant incline at SH541505, the much decayed formation contour chases to SH546493 where, having passed through a cutting, the line from Prince of Wales quarry is met near that quarry's mill. From here on the condition of the formation improves and can be followed most of the way to the triangular junction at SH552441 near Braich y Bib. The formation from Gorseddau quarry which joins here is mainly a clearly defined track with the final few yards as road.

From the junction the line is clearly traceable to another junction at Ynysypandy mill (SH550433). Shortly beyond are faint traces of a branch to the east which may have been for peat gathering.

Near Henfail at SH533419 a short, nicely portalled tunnel takes the line under a road. From here it is less well defined to SH527412 where it crossed the A4871 on the level. Beyond there are only intermittent traces to the now almost invisible western portal of the short tunnel under the A4871 at SH546406. The line is obvious behind the village of Penmorfa where it passes traces of small quarries, of which one, Tyn y Llan (SH554406) was connected. At Tremadog the route passes the present Primary School but the switchback reversing loop where it dropped to main road level has been lost under housing. The route to Porthmadog alongside the canal (Y Cyt) is obvious. The actual crossing of the main road where it entered what is now the Welsh Highland Railway car park has been lost, but a stile defines the site of the level crossing of the main line railway.

Having run beside what is now Madoc Street West, the original Gorseddau swung south to run along Madoc Street. As rebuilt in the 1870s the line did not go down Madoc Street but carried on almost straight along what is now a lane, past Richard Williams slate works (opposite and a little further on than the present monumental masons), to join and use the Croesor (later W.H.R.) line outside the flour mill, through the present car park to unite with the original route at the south end of Madoc Street, which crossed High Street, reaching the wharves via the present Ffestiniog Railway car park. This swing round through the car park was probably the route taken by the early Tremadoc Tramway.

In about 1903, the 2'g 1880 Moel y Gest (stone) quarry tramway to Porthmadog station was extended to run through what is now the main line railway car park to join and make use of the then abandoned Gorseddau formation to reach the Croesor and the F.R. to the harbour. This odd line with its Falcon vertical boiler and cylinder loco thus passed over four differently owned tracks in about two miles! The line was abandoned when the quarry closed in 1907 and when it reopened in 1919 a standard gauge siding was laid to the foot of the incline, this siding being lifted post WW2.

HENDRE DDU TRAMWAY (SH804124 to 846100. 2' 6"g. Horse/I.C.) *c.1868-1939. Coed Cwm Caws forestry branch revived during WW2. Some use of the branch from Maes y Gamfa quarry (SH818127) post WW2.*
The main line running from the foot of the Hendre Ddu quarry incline, now forms the valley road. At SH823112 the site of the short Gartheiniog spur has been lost in roadworks but the line of the tramway past the nearby quarry mill

building is obvious. The old incline from the quarry has been lost in forestry, but the newer, lower route via a (collapsed) tunnel is clear. A few yards further on, beyond the stream, the Maes y Gamfa branch is quite apparent, and can be easily followed to the exit incline of that quarry (SH818127). Part way along this branch, there was reputedly an incline connection with Talymieryn quarry (SH825119).

There is some trace of the Coed y Chwarel branch which left the main line at SH842104 to serve the quarry at SH830095. At Aberangell the formation leaves the road to swing across fields to the site of the exchange siding at Aberangell station. Less obvious is the original route which ran north west almost opposite the Coed y Chwarel branch to run behind the village to near the village school and back by a reversing loop to the station. A short length, still obvious, was retained to serve a tiny brickworks.

Slight vestiges of a spur south to Nant Hir farm and another north to Cefn Gwyn farm emphasise the social uses of the line, as does the fact that the Coed y Chwarel branch also served Cwmllecoediog Hall.

There are also vestiges of the WW1 timber branches. One ran south west from SH832104 and a short one north from SH838105.

JOHN ROBINSON TRAMWAY (SH515548 to 498539. 3' 6"g. Horse) *1868 – c.1875.*
The road defines the route from the Fron/Old Braich quarries to Y Fron. There the line swung west and the branch from (New) Braich quarry (SH510552) joined. This branch is defined by a margin alongside the Braich access road.

At Y Fron common trace is lost before becoming a surfaced road, off which can be seen the formation of the link to the Cilgwyn Horseshoe which latterly enabled that quarry to reach the N.W.N.G.R. At the end of the road, beyond Bryntwrog Terrace, the route continues as a track, first across open moorland, then behind Cilgwyn quarry between stone walls which enclose what were quarrymen's smallholdings. At SH498541 are traces of the incline down to Talysarn quarry (SH496534).

LLANBERIS BRANCH (SH482618 to 580601. S.G.) *1869-1930 (regular passengers), Freight 1964.*
Much of the line from the site of the junction south of Caernarfon, now lost in roadworks, can be readily traced. Immediately beyond the now disused road bridge over the Seiont are the abutments of the bridge of a branch to the Glanmorfa writing slate factory (now Schofields). Ahead a housing road defines the brickworks sub-branch, whilst a works road defines the actual route. It is not practicable to follow the two miles to Pont Rhug station, since there were seven crossings of the Seiont. Part way along at Llanbeblig modern industrial buildings occupy both sides of the river. Those on the eastern bank are on the site of the original Peblig flour mill, converted to a woollen mill in 1861 and used as an outlier for Hunting Aviation's WW2 Llanberis factory. On the opposite bank, served by a tramway was the Peblig brickworks. After yet another crossing of the river and after passing under a road, it approaches the Padarn Railway formation at SH534643 and parallels it for just over half a mile. Here between the two railways, factories processed block brought in both on the Padarn line and this Llanberis branch. At Pont Rhythallt where there are remains of a station, it yet again crossed the river and from here the two lines separate to pass on either side of Llyn Padarn. At Cwm y Glo the trackbed and the station have been absorbed by road improvements, and except for a mile from SH564615 to 577607 much of the rest of the route now forms the Llanberis by-pass. There is virtually no trace of the sidings which served the foot of the Ffridd incline (or indeed the lower part of that incline) or the Glynrhonwy quarry sidings (including the WW2 loop sidings for the Air Ministry).

Buildings of the Glynrhonwy Lower quarry have been incorporated into the present factories at SH572602. The surviving stretch of the railway bed forms a pleasant walk, with at one point a nice accommodation bridge over.

Llanberis passenger station is in re-use, and streets define where a line from Goodmans quarry (SH572606) ran to the station and on to tip into the lake.

MAENCLOCHOG RAILWAY (SN102197 to 077303. S.G.) *1876-1882, 1884-1888, 1895 (to SM936320 Letterston), 1899 to Fishguard, closures during WW1 & WW2. – 1949 (Letterston-Letterston Junction closed 1965.*
Substantially all of the line from its junction west of Clunderwen to Rosebush quarry is readily traceable, the final stretch now forming a road. The extension (the North Pembrokeshire Railway) from a point south east of Rosebush village, through the somewhat imaginatively restored Rosebush station to Letterston junction (SM937320) is also well defined, and can be followed with varying degrees of difficulty.

MAWDDWY RAILWAY (SH820045 to 859140. S.G.) *1867-1931 (Passengers), Goods 1950. (Part closures 1905-1909.) A short (½ mile) stretch from the terminus used 1975/76 for unsuccessful 2' gauge tourist line.*
The trackbed is obvious from its junction at Cemaes Road via Cemaes to Aberangell. There are the abutments of an overbridge, one of the line's few engineering features and also traces of the exchange sidings of the Hendre Ddu Tramway. There are scant remains of Mallwyd halt but the terminus building and the engine shed at Dinas Mawddwy are in reuse as a tearoom and workshop respectively.

MOEL SIABOD TRAMWAY (SH717556 to 735571. 2'g. Horse/Gravity) *c.1862-1951.*
From the foot of the Foel quarry exit incline the line is traceable partly over boggy ground for a mile to the head of a long shallow incline at SH727563. Part way down this incline a level formation runs in from Rhos quarry and, via this connection, Rhos continued to use the line after Foel closed in the early 1880s. At the foot of this incline are two steep pitches down to the road, separated by a manoeuvring loop. There was a further short pitch to a mill at the riverside but little trace of this remains. The dwellings on the road are quarry-related, but the neat little warehouse belonged to Penrhiw, a hone quarry at SH722540.

NANTLLE RAILWAY (SH508535 to 478625, later 470543, later 488529. 3' 6"g. Horse) *1828-1963 (surviving section east of Talysarn)*
From Penyrorsedd quarry to Talysarn station the route and its various diversions is readily followed, much now forming a rudimentary roadway. Close to the foot of the Penyrorsedd exit incline, the stables and water-wheel powered fodder cutting shed are ruinous and overgrown. Near this end of the formation there is, unusually for north Wales, a fine run of stone sleeper blocks.

West of Talysarn the main road occupies the common trackbed of the Nantlle line and the L. & N.W.R. A hundred yards short of the cross roads at Penygroes, the trackbed of the S.G. railway swings south while the north-curving route of the Nantlle is defined by County Road and, beyond the main road, by the narrow 'Tram Road' lane, most of the way to Tyddyn Bengam. Here united with the trackbed of the Caernarfon-Afonwen line it forms a cycle track which passes immediately alongside the revived Welsh Highland Dinas station.

At Bontnewydd a fine bridge over the Afon Beuno survives. From there the formations slightly deviate several times from the later railway until they reach Coed Helen tunnel (SH482616). From here the route, including the Seiont bridge, is unclear until is defined by the road to the Slate Quays.

NORTH WALES NARROW GAUGE RAILWAY
(SH571526 to 477586. 2'g. Steam) *1877 – Closed passengers, Bryngwyn branch 1913, main line 1916. Absorbed by W.H.R. 1922.*
At the time of writing, track is being relaid, thus altering some archaeological features.

At Rhyd Ddu (latterly South Snowdon) a public lavatory is on the site of the once extensive station buildings. From there the whole of the line to Dinas can be readily and almost continuously traced. The first feature along the formation is the incline from Rhos Clogwyn quarry (SH576530) and vestiges of the ropeway which provided the Welsh Highland with its last slate cargoes. The incline down from Glanrafon quarry (SH581540) which was the source of most of the tonnage carried by the N.W.N.G.R. 'main line', is a prominent feature, just beyond it the line crossed the Treweunydd gorge by an iron bridge which was by far the biggest piece of engineering of the line.

Shortly after Llyn Cwellyn the line crossed under the road and just beyond is the site of a siding and a possible tramway from Plas y Nant quarry (SH552562). Apart from two river crossings, the line is less well defined to near Betws Garmon church, just short of which was a spur and level crossing to the Garreg Fawr iron mine (SH540575).

Having crossed under the road and again over the river, at Betws Garmon station the formation of the tramway from Hafod y Wern quarry (SH530571) is evident. Beyond is the prominent formation of a branch apparently intended to serve the iron mine but which was connected to Treflan slate quarry (SH539584) and possibly Garreg Fawr quarry (SH538582).

Just beyond Waunfawr station where a siding served the Dudley Park granite quarry (the limit of track at time of writing), the line crossed under the road and followed the river in a gradual curve to Tryfan junction at SH502592. From there the line made its way downhill southwesterly, with several stream and road crossings, to pass under the Caernarfon-Porthmadog road and curve into Dinas station. The site of the original N.G. track is now cleared as a car park, the relaid line running through the station on the S.G. trackbed.

The now much overgrown Bryngwyn branch left Tryfan junction, where there are vestiges of the station building, in a tight curve to run southwest to Rhostryfan station (SH498579), which is defined by a row of garages. The in-filled cutting where the line passed under the road is obvious, from there the line is less clear as it snaked for almost a mile up to Bryngwyn station (SH498561). From here the Bryngwyn incline is boldly prominent to Drumhead at SH506558. Of the four branches, the northerly one curving its sinuous path to Alexandra quarry (SH519562) forms a trackway. The easterly branch runs more directly, via an incline to Alexandra's close neighbour, Moel Tryfan quarry (SH515559). The south easterly branch to Braich quarry (SH510552) is less clear although the inclines down to the branch are in good condition. The southerly branch winding its way through Fron village to Fron quarry (SH515548) is more obvious and at one point in the village, rail is on the ground. Defined by a rough track, is the connection across to the Cilgwyn 'horseshoe' line which latterly enabled that quarry to dispatch via the N.W.N.G.R. Railway.

OERNANT TRAMWAY (SJ188481 to 207435. 3'g. Horse/gravity) *1856-1900s.*
This is easily followed from Moelyfaen quarry (SJ185477) to Clogau (SJ185463) where it now forms the access road to this working quarry. At Clogau there was a pre-tramway incline

to the road as well as the actual tramway incline which is followed by an almost flat trackway to the head of the fine main incline, with vestiges of the unusual drumhouse where the brakeman was above the drum to have a clear view down the incline. From the foot of incline there are traces to near the telephone box at Abbey Farm, where it crossed the main road. From there, it is at least partly traceable to the embanked section approaching Pentrefelin. The Pentrefelin slate mill is now in reuse as a museum. To the east of it, a cleared space occupies the site of the G.W.R. slate sidings.

PADARN RAILWAY (DINORWIG QUARRIES RAILWAY) (SH593599 [later 586604] to 527679. 4'g. Steam) *1843 – Workmen's trains from 1895 to 1947, closed 1962.*
The route of the narrow gauge feeder around Glan y Bala now forms the road to the pumped storage station and the approach to the Slate Museum. Glan y Bala tunnel is sealed but intact.

The trackbed alongside Llyn Padarn from Gilfach Ddu to Pen y Llyn has since 1971 been re-used by the 2'g Llanberis Lake Railway. (It was originally intended that this would run right around the lake, utilising the trackbed of the Llanberis branch.)

At Pen y Llyn the formation passes under the road and again at Pont Rhythallt. From there it runs closely alongside the S.G. Llanberis Branch separated by slate factories. After passing under a road, it swings northward away from the standard gauge.

The route is fairly clear to Bethel level crossing, just before which are the ruins of a carriage shed and a footbridge. Beyond Bethel the line becomes increasingly difficult to follow, until is passes under a road at SH536677. From here, swinging west as a lane, it passes railway housing still in occupation, a carriage shed, engine shed, and a small building partly made of the original stone sleeper blocks.

Regrettably this lane ends abruptly where the Port Dinorwig by-pass destroyed the fine Penscoins drumhouse at SH532678 where the quarry-gauge trucks were taken off the transporters and crewled down to the port.

At the dock, the mouth of the tunnel which carried the incline under the main road is extant.

PENRHYN RAILROAD (Tramway) (SH615663 to 592726. 2'g. Horse) *1801-1876.*

The actual start has been lost under subsequent work but from Coed y Parc it shows clearly as a lane crossing a road on the level at SH614665. The route running north is clear, with the subsequent steam railway merging from the right. With the old and new lines on a common bed, after about a mile, this, the old line, dropped away down the Cilgeraint incline.

From here to the Dinas incline, except for a cutting, traces are sparse, but the incline itself is discernible near Dinas farm. The top of a buried arch shows where the incline passed under the road. The route is partly traceable alongside the river, but once north of the A55 the route is very clear, becoming a byroad at Bryn near Llandygái.

The route is then lost under the Llandygái Industrial Estate but at SH594714 the underpass (rebuilt) is still open. The route followed the curve of the Penrhyn estate wall to the head of Marchogion incline. The incline drumhouse, now in reuse was a complex building including living accommodation, stables, and in the days when it formed part of the Llandygái tramway, a horse-whim haulage.

At the foot of the incline the line turns to cross the Cegin by a single arched bridge before swinging round to pass (with remarkably little headroom!) under the shared formation of the later steam line and the standard gauge branch. It then re-crosses the Cegin by a three arched stone bridge after which the trackbed becomes merged with that of the steam line.

Although the route of the original Llandygái tramway has been lost under the 'Model Village', traces of the incline down to the flint mill on the Ogwen are extant immediately south of the main line railway at SH600706.

PENRHYN RAILWAY (SH615663 to 592726. 2'g. Steam) *1876, workmen's trains to 1951. Closed 1962.*
The line began at Coed y Parc, which like Dinorwig's Gilfach Ddu was a central workshop, plus in this case slate factories.

It left Coed y Parc on a slate embankment, crossing over a byroad at Cilgeraint. It shortly merged with the earlier tramway (which had crossed the byroad on the level) and ran on, via alternate cuttings and embankment, to the multi-way level crossing at Hen Durnpike. From there the route is mostly obvious, particularly where it runs between walls or on a cut shelf, making a tight almost 180 degree loop to the site of a bridge over a road. After crossing on a brick arch, the trackbed of the Bethesda branch far below the line entered Tregarth and, in a cutting, passes under a road. After briefly running alongside the S.G. Bethesda Branch, it passes under a farm access lane before curving north into woodland and onto an embankment. The B4366 was crossed by a viaduct but now only the south abutment remains. Rejoining the Bethesda branch in the Cegin valley, it passed under its skewed bridge.

Beyond the A55 it runs alongside the Cegin roughly paralleling the Bethesda Branch, which curves away to join the main line, while the Penrhyn goes under the fine main line Cegin viaduct. It is now more difficult to follow through the narrowing valley until the S.G. Port Branch merges in from the right. Both pass under the main road and cross and re-cross the river by common bridges. The actual access to the port area is blocked but beyond, the fine bridge which carried the dock road over this line and the port branch is still in use.

PORT DINORWIG SIDING (SH532681 to 525678. S.G.)
1852-1961.
At the port end particularly, the formation is overgrown. The original dock and the ship repair basin are extant as a marina with some buildings of the ship repairing yard remaining. The 'new' dock has been filled and is now a housing estate. The rail tracks, narrow gauge, standard gauge and 7' (for the crane), have all been lifted.

PORT PENRHYN BRANCH (SH591709 to 592726. S.G.)
1852-1963.
Readily traceable throughout its length including, near the port, the bridges over the Cegin which were widened to accommodate the Penrhyn steam line. This sharing of structures is a reminder that the branch was Penrhyn, not railway property. At the port itself, although all trackwork has vanished, most of the buildings including the office, engine shed and the multi-seater lavatory remain. Of the significant structures only the writing slate factory, which during the 1920s was operated by E.J.J. Dixon of Bangor as a slate factory and afterwards was a foundry unconnected with the quarry, has failed to survive. It is to the great credit of the Penrhyn estate that they have resisted the inappropriate developments which now disfigure other redundant slate ports.

RATGOED TRAMWAY (SH780120 to 770098. 2' 3"g. Horse/gravity) *1859 – c.1950.*
This started at the lower mill of Ratgoed quarry. Its course down valley, now a rough road, passes various diggings of Cymerau quarry, crossing the stream at the site of Cymerau mill (SH779116). Acting as a forestry road, the formation passes the extensive Cymerau tips, before joining the Aberllefeni-Aberangell road. Its course is obvious, crossing and re-crossing that road to reach Aberllefenni station by way of the mill pond dam.

RHIWBACH TRAMWAY (SH737460 to 702459. 2'g. Horse – i.c.) *1863 – c.1953. (to foot of upper (No 3) incline. From foot of middle (No 2) incline to F.R. Duffws 1963. Foot of No 3 to foot of No 2 1976.)*
The summit section is continuous and clear from the head of the incline up from Rhiwbach quarry. The line and reversing loop down from Bwlch y Slaters quarry joins at a gate at SH732460. Beyond the head of Blaen y Cwm quarry incline (SH733463) and the Cwt y Bugail junction (SH732467) the trackbed becomes boggy. A culvert preserves the path past the washed-out Bowydd bridge to the head of the incline system down to Blaenau through Maenofferen (SH715467) and Bowydd (SH708462) quarries. The upper and lower inclines are passable as are the inter-incline stretches. No 2 incline has some track on the ground and some drumhouse gear in situ but is totally overgrown.

SOUTH SNOWDON TRAMWAY (SH612525 to 627512. 2'g. Horse/gravity) *1868-1880s.*
At the Hafod y Llan quarry a path defines an earlier tramway which ran the few yards to the trackway. On the other side of the stream the actual Hafod y Llan tramway occupies a fine and well engineered formation to the head of the upper incline, itself a fine landscape feature. On the way an embankment cuts the steep, pre-existing Braich yr Oen copper mine tramway whose stone sleeper blocks are clearly visible.

Near the foot of the upper incline are the abutments of a bridge over the access track. There is a well defined level section to the head of the lower incline which ran down to the stables and stores at valley floor level. These now form part of Hafod y Llan farm and still await the arrival of the long promised railway.

TALYLLYN RAILWAY (SH678068 [later 681067] to 586005. 2' 3"g. Steam) *1866. Traffic from quarry ceased 1946. Village branch closed c.1950.*
The line has been extended from its original terminus to a new one at Nantcol at the foot of the Alltwyllt incline, this stretch having originally been part of the quarry tramway rather than the actual railway. The inclines now form a fine, if steep footpath to and through Bryneglwys quarry.

Of the Village branch, the overgrown, slate slabbed incline formation is extant although all trace has gone of the unique drumhouse which straddled the running line. At the foot of incline it takes the eye of faith to connect the modern buildings with the smithy, writing slate factory (later a sawmill) etc. The lines which ran at the back of Llanegryn and Water streets, with spurs to Jerusalem chapel, the school etc. have all gone.

Near Towyn, Pendre station with its well-equipped workshops is little altered but at Wharf station there have been considerable alterations although the original layout of the exchange with the standard gauge is clear.

TALYSARN SUB-BRANCH (SH467529 to 488529. S.G.) *1872-1963.*
Route is reasonably visible from Penygroes station curving south and east to cross the A4085 south of the village to join the road to Talysarn which occupies the Nantlle Railway trackbed. At Talysarn the site of the station and 3'-SG exchange sidings is obvious.

TANAT VALLEY LIGHT RAILWAY (SJ250229 to 054262. S.G.) *1904-1951 (Passengers). Goods beyond Llanrhaeadr 1952, to Llanrhaeadr 1960.*
The trackbed meanders from Llanymynech to Llangynog almost as if deliberately avoiding the villages which it served. With a minimum of engineering and the buildings being exiguous structures, there are few remains. There are

vestiges at most stations, particularly, Llangynog where there are traces of the Craig Rhiwarth quarry track formation at the incline foot, although the tunnel under the road is now obscured.

TYDDYN SIEFFRE TRAMWAY (SH629134 to 634151. 2'g? Horse/gravity) *c.1858, ceased as quarry line before 1895, being used from that date to c.1900 for passengers to a housing development.*
At the foot of an incline from the quarry, the line crosses the road at the War Memorial at SH630135. Its line to the wharf is clearly defined as is the later diversion to the Cambrian Railways erstwhile triangular junction.

UPPER CORRIS TRAMWAY (SH744089 to 754066 2' 3"g.) *1859-1930.*
From SH744089, its route down to Corris is partially defined by a path. The connection with Abercwmeiddaw quarry, (SH746093) is obvious, but the Ty'n y Berth (SH738087) spur is less clear. The tunnel from Gaewern (SH745086) is buried under road improvements, but the incline and abutments of the bridge over the Deri from Abercorris quarry (SH754089) survive. At Braich Goch (SH748079), the mills area has been tipped over to form the visitor centre, car park, etc. The access tunnel to 'King Arthur's Caverns' represents the level of the mill yard and the tramway route. Beyond the Monument where the line squeezed between dwellings and the road, little accommodation bridges survive. The Braich Goch Hotel car park occupies the trackbed which is traceable to its junction at Maespoeth.

Of the planned extension to Glyn Iago (SH719072), the head of a part-built incline down to Upper Corris is at SH727084, between there and the quarry a forestry road has been built on the trackbed.

WELSH HIGHLAND RAILWAY (SH477586 to 569385 2'g.) *1923-1936/7.* From SH477586 to 571526 see N.W.N.G.R. From SH608428 to 569385 see Croesor.

Dinas to Rhyd Ddu as North Wales Narrow Gauge. South from Rhyd Ddu until the drop down through Beddgelert Forest, the route is obvious with a nice bridge under the main road near the summit of the line at Pitt's Head (SH575515) where some deviations from the less direct Portmadoc, Beddgelert & South Snowdon route can be seen.

In the forest down to the looping curve at the Hafod Ruffydd picnic site the route is defined by a forestry road, some deviations both of the P.B. & S.S. and of the timber-working tracks are discernible. The route is less clear in the vicinity of the caravan site but at Cwm Cloch immediately east of Beddgelert the magnificent Cwm Cloch 'alpine' looping curve is a prominent feature, cutting through the steeper, more direct P.B. & S.S. formations.

At Beddgelert station is a water tower pillar and the base of the small G.G.I. station building. South from there the formation enters a 43 yard tunnel beyond which the never-used P.B. & S.S. bridge crosses the main road, pointing towards the wingwalls of the accommodation bridge through an embankment that was never built.

The W.H.R. swung right, past the cemetery, and under the road to cross the river by the Bryn y Felin bridge (removed 1999). On the eastern bank it met the P.B. & S.S. formation, which runs some distance north towards Nant Gwynant, past traces of the bridge by which the P.B. & S.S. would have crossed the river. The W.H.R. turned south, through the Glaslyn pass via three tunnels, of 37 yards, 17 yards and 300 yards, to cross Cwm Bychan by an embankment which is pierced by a nice arch bridge. After a cutting it crosses over the road at Nantmor (where there was a siding and a tiny station building) and then skirts what was in pre-Cob days the wooded shoreline of the Glaslyn estuary. It then runs on a shallow embankment to join the

Croesor at SH608428. From there on the route was as the Croesor except for the W.H.R. Portmadoc New station immediately south of the crossing of the main line. Of this only the water tower pillars remain. (The whole of the route is scheduled to be relaid, in anticipation of which all bridges south of Beddgelert other than the road overbridge at Nanmor were removed in 2000.)

WHITLAND & CARDIGAN, formerly Whitland & Taf Vale. (SM167184 to 180457. S.G.) *1873/85-1962/3.*
Interrupted in places by fencing and development, it can be intermittently followed from its junction near Clunderwen to the now reused side of Cardigan station. Northwest of Cilgerran a stretch forms the access road to the West Wales Wildlife Centre. Most station buildings are in re-use.

The siding into Glogue quarry (SN220328) and the Pencelli incline and siding at (SN191278) are traceable but the one feeder line, the ¾ mile 2' 6"g Penlan tramway east from Rhyd Owen (SN196285) is now overgrown.

Some Minor Tramways

BRYN GLAS (SH731423 to 727421. 2'g? Horse) *Early 1900s.*
A track defines this ephemeral ¼ mile line to the road, built during the brief upsurge caused by the 1900-1903 Penrhyn dispute.

FOEL GRON (SH744428 to 746425. 2'g? Horse?) *1860-c.1900.*
This ¼ mile line proved remarkably durable for a remote and marginal working. Its route from the quarry to the road is still well defined, but the little mill at its end has succumbed to road widening.

LLANFFLEWIN (SH347892 to 349901. g? Horse?) *1875-1800?*
During the mid 1870s the advances in slate prices and increases in demand were being extravagantly extrapolated, resulting in grandiose but unrealistic excavations. A fine causeway of waste rock defines this short-lived ½ mile line from such quarry to a road.

Some Notable Tramway Incline Relics

The most spectacular is the zig-zag formation of the six-pitch **Moelwyn incline** (from SH661443 to the Ffestiniog Railway) which dropped more than 1000'. The lower ends of the converging highest inclines are lost in Llyn Stwlan as is the top end of the second pitch down to the site of the mill. The formations of the further four pitches down to the old trackbed of the Ffestiniog Railway are intact.

Less prominent but even longer was the **Graig Ddu incline** cascade (SH724454 to the Ffestiniog & Blaenau Railway), falling almost 1400'. The topmost (internal) incline has been quarried away but the main pitch down to the secondary mill site at Dŵr Oer and the two further pitches to road level are extant. The final pitch down to the railway has been lost in housing development.

Also in the Blaenau area and a feeder to the F.R. is the **Wrysgan incline** (SH678456 to the F.R.), its fall of 700' in a single pitch is only exceeded by the **Rhosydd** and the **Croesor** inclines (SH658464 and SH657455 respectively) to the Croesor Tramway, it is notable for its steepness and being partly in tunnel. Other than the lowest end, the formation is intact.

Another grand feature is the **Pant Mawr** 2 pitch incline formation dropping 900' from SH649450 to the Croesor Tramway. Interestingly the upper pitch was abandoned and the lower extended to be used by the **Fron Boeth** quarry via the unique SH644451 – 646446 tunnel, the southern end of which is open.

Most of the **Ffridd incline** at Llanberis is readily traceable from its head at SH553602 almost to the site of the L. & N.W.R. sidings 800' below. The two upper pitches, were self-acting, the third pitch was, due to its length, steam-powered single acting. Many of the tracks whereby the numerous separate quarries reached the incline are traceable.

Other extant incline formations include **Penarth** from SJ108424 to the Ruabon-Dolgellau Railway, **Glanrafon** from SH581540 to the North Wales Narrow Gauge Railway, Nyth y Gigfran (SH690462) and Hafodlas (SH780562), as well as the many internal incline systems, outside the scope of this book.

Miscellaneous slate-related railway archaeology

G.W.R. RHUABON-BARMOUTH JUNCTION (S.G.) *1868-1965/68.*
Part reopened as Llangollen Railway, part of the trackbed utilised for narrow gauge Bala Lake Railway.

Pentrefelin (SJ218436). Between the railway and the canal at the termination of the Oernant Tramway, the slate sawing mill is now a motor museum, to the east of which were sidings.

Apart from about 2 miles occupied by the Dolgellau by-pass, the route is almost continuously traceable.

MANCHESTER & MILFORD RAILWAY (Carmarthen & Cardigan Railway S.G.) *1860/67-1965.*
Part reopened as Gwili Railway, part of trackbed used by narrow gauge Vale of Teifi Railway.

At Penygraigygigfran (SN419326), widening of formation denotes site of siding, or proposed siding, serving a short tramway from the adjacent slate quarry.

Survivors

The original standard gauge line, the erstwhile Chester & Holyhead Railway, is still with us, having seen almost all its imitators, rivals and successors, come and go. The Newtown-Machynlleth and the Aberystwyth & Welch Coast carries on as the Cambrian Coast Railway, its durability a tribute to the acumen and foresight of Messrs. Davies and Savin. Due to the dedication of enthusiasts we still have the Talyllyn, the Ffestiniog and the Welsh Highland, and something of the Corris. They, and the non-slate narrow gauge lines such as the Welshpool & Llanfair, the Rheidol and the re-created tourist lines, ensure the survival in steam of a number of historic slate locomotives and continue and develop the railway engineering technology which evolved in the service of Welsh slate.

Index

Selected published bibliography

Anon, *A Return to Corris*, Avon-Anglia, 1988.

Barrie, D.S.M., *A Regional History of the Railways of G.B. Vol 12*, David & Charles, 1980.

Baugham, P.E., *ditto, Vol 11*, David & Charles, 1980.

Bingley, W.A., *A Journal of a Tour through North Wales, etc.*, London, 1797.

Boyd, J.I.C., *Narrow Gauge Railways in Mid Wales*, Oakwood, 1970.

Boyd, J.I.C., *Narrow Gauge Railways in South Caernarvonshire*, Oakwood, 1972.

Boyd, J.I.C., *The Festiniog Railways Vols 1 & 2*, Oakwood, 1975.

Boyd, J.I.C., *Narrow Gauge Railways in North Caernarvonshire Vols 1, 2 & 3*, Oakwood, 1981/6.

Boyd, J.I.C., *Tal-y-Llyn Railway*, Wild Swan, 1988.

Bradley, V.J., *Industrial Locos of N Wales*, Ind Rly Soc, 1992.

Carrington, D.C., *Delving in Dinorwig*, Gwasg Carreg Gwalch, 1994.

Christiansen, R., *The Forgotten Railways of North & Mid Wales*, David & Charles, 1976.

Cozens, L., *The Corris Railway*, Cozens, 1949.

Davies, D.L., *The Glyn Valley Tramway*, Oakwood, 1962.

Davies, John, *A History of Wales*, Allen Lane, 1993.

Eames, Aled, *The Twilight of Welsh Sail*, University of Wales Press, 1984.

Eames, Aled, *Shrouded Quays*, Gwasg Carreg Gwalch, 1991.

Eames, Aled, *Heb Long wrth y Cei*, Gwasg Carreg Gwalch, 1991.

Elis-Williams, M., *Bangor Port of Beaumaris*, Gwynedd Arch. Serv., 1988.

Foster, C Le Neve, *Ore & Stone Mining*, Griffin, 1910.

Green, C.C., *North Wales Branch Line Album*, I Allan, 1983.

Green, C.C., *Coast Lines of the Cambrian Railways*, Wild Swan, 1993.

Holmes, A., *Slates from Abergynolwyn*, Gwynedd A. S., 1986.

Hughes & Eames, *Porthmadog Ships*, Gwynedd Arch. Serv., 1975.

Hughes, H.D., *Hynafiaethau Llandegai & Llanllechid*, Argraffdy Arfon, 1979.

Jones, I.W., *Eagles Do Not Catch Flies*, J.W. Greaves, 1986.

Johnson, P., *The Welsh Narrow Gauge Railways*, Railway World, 1991.

Jones, R.J., *Felinheli*, Bridge Books, 1992.

Jones & Hatherill, *Llechwedd & Other Ffestiniog Railways*, Quarry Tours, 1977.

Lee, C., *The Welsh Highland Railway*, Welsh Highland Railway, 1970.

Lee, C., *The Penrhyn Railway*, Welsh Highland Railway, 1972.

Lewis, M.J.T., *How Ffestiniog Got Its Railway*, Railway & Canal Historical Society, 1968.

Lewis, M.J.T., *Early Wooden Railways*, R.K.P., 1970.

Lewis & Denton, *Rhosydd Slate Quarry*, Cottage Press, 1974.

Lloyd, Lewis, *The Port of Caernarfon 1793-1900*, Lloyd, 1989.

Lloyd, Lewis, *Pwllheli, The Port & Mart of Llŷn*, Lloyd, 1991.

Lloyd, Lewis, *Wherever Freights May Offer*, Lloyd, 1993.

Lloyd, Lewis, *De Winton's of Caernarfon*, Lloyd, 1994.

Lloyd, Lewis, *A Real Little Seaport*, Lloyd, 1996.

Mitchell & Eyres, *The Talyllyn Railway*, Past & Present Pubs., 1996.

Mitchell & Smith, *Branch Lines around P'madog*, Middleton, 1993.

Morris, Richard, *The Archaeology of Railways*, Tempus Publishing, 1999.

Owen-Jones, S., *Railways of Wales*, National Museum, 1981.

Richards, A.J., *Slate Quarrying at Corris*, Gwasg Carreg Gwalch, 1994.

Richards, A.J., *Slate Quarrying in Wales*, Gwasg Carreg Gwalch, 1995.

Richards, A.J., *The Slate Quarries of Pembrokeshire*, Gwasg Carreg Gwalch, 1998.

Richards, A.J., *The Slate Regions of North & Mid Wales*, Gwasg Carreg Gwalch, 1999.

Turner, S., *The Padarn & Penrhyn Railways*, David & Charles, 1975.

Wren, W.J., *The Tanat Valley*, David & Charles, 1968.